Kate Kramer

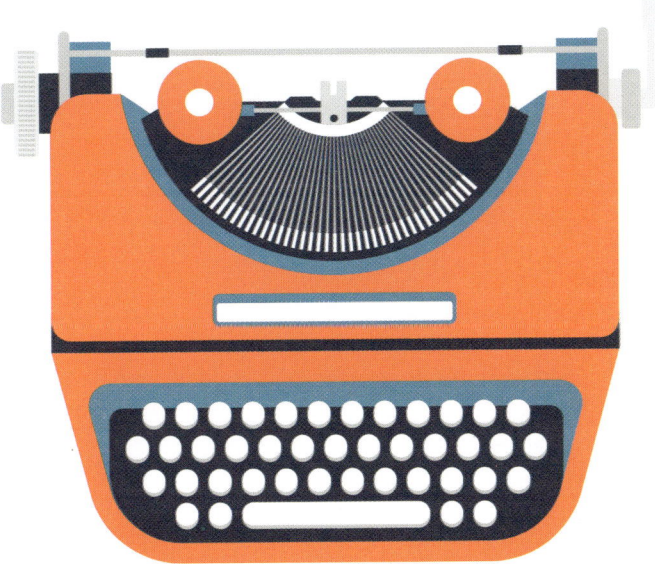

Artists Write to Work

A Practical Guide to Writing about Your Art

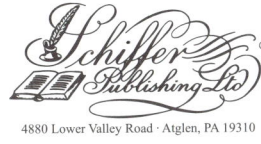

4880 Lower Valley Road · Atglen, PA 19310

Cover design by John Cheek
Type set in Bitter

ISBN: 978-0-7643-5649-0
Printed in China

Published by Schiffer Publishing, Ltd.
4880 Lower Valley Road
Atglen, PA 19310
Phone: (610) 593-1777; Fax: (610) 593-2002
E-mail: Info@schifferbooks.com
Web: www.schifferbooks.com

For our complete selection of fine books on this and related subjects, please visit our website at www.schifferbooks.com. You may also write for a free catalog.

Schiffer Publishing's titles are available at special discounts for bulk purchases for sales promotions or premiums. Special editions, including personalized covers, corporate imprints, and excerpts, can be created in large quantities for special needs. For more information, contact the publisher.

We are always looking for people to write books on new and related subjects. If you have an idea for a book, please contact us at proposals@schifferbooks.com.

For Christopher, Charlotte, and Theo
for making the world a better, more beautiful place

Contents

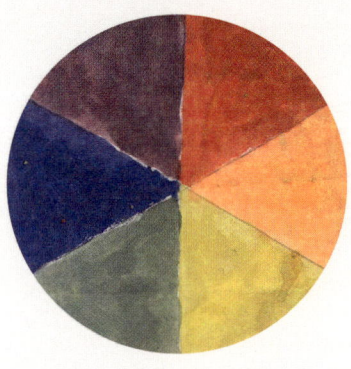

Acknowledgments

This primer, a distillation of about twenty-five years of personal and professional experience in the arts and humanities, is my way to pay it forward. In a way, it's an homage to those who shared the wealth of their experience and knowledge with me along the way. Richard Weedman, Helaine Fendelman, Christopher Poehlmann, Valerie Ross, and Merry Weisner-Hanks have gone above and beyond over the years. The artists, former students, gallerists, and writers who generously contributed to this volume deserve a special thank-you as well: Rochelle Weiner, Wendy and Marvin Hill, Fred Tieken, Lauren Purje, Caroline Dy, Morgan Dummitt, Greg Biché, Michael Davidson, Jason Rohlf, Greg Klassen, Henry Klimowicz, Carolina Hernandez Beltran, Steve Minicola, Theresa Abel, and my darlings Charlotte and Theo. Both the Barnes Foundation (Philadelphia, Pennsylvania) and the Utah Division of Arts also graciously granted permission to reprint materials. Finally: I thank Peter Schiffer and his publishing team for believing in this project and for bringing this writing guide for artists into print!

Theo Poehlmann. *Color Wheel*, 2015. Watercolor on paper.
Photo credit © 2017 Christopher Poehlmann

Introduction

Artists write. Every day.

It might not be the favorite activity that gets them humming in the studio, but they write. Every day.

Artists write blogs, emails, and posts to websites and social media. Daily. They also periodically write agreements, applications, and proposals, along with the ever-important cover letters. To support these written agreements, applications, and proposals, artists write artist biographies, resumes, and statements. Regularly.

Craft and fine artists practice a range of specialties. Following the Bureau of Labor Statistics' (US Department of Labor) lead, this volume uses the term *artist* to reference a wide variety of creatives: cartoonists, ceramic artists, fiber artists, fine art painters, furniture makers, glass artists, illustrators, jewelry artists, medical and scientific illustrators, public artists, printmakers, sculptors, sketch artists, tattoo artists, and video artists.[1] Designers would (should!) be included in this list as well. In addition, the BLS provides this interesting nugget of information:

> In addition to selling their artwork, many artists have at least one other job to support their craft or art careers. Some artists work in museums or art galleries as art directors or as archivists, curators, or museum workers, planning and setting up exhibits. Others teach craft or art classes or conduct workshops in schools or in their own studios. For more information on workers who teach art classes, see the profiles on kindergarten and elementary-school teachers, middle-school teachers, high-school teachers, and postsecondary teachers. (www.bls.gov/ooh/arts-and-design/craft-and-fine-artists.htm#tab-2. Accessed May 23, 2017.)

For anyone looking for day jobs related to their art, the Bureau of Labor Statistics provides a wide range of options to investigate. It also provides standard incomes and forecasts job growth.

The student who went to art school to avoid writing might think that writing to work is going to be a real drag.[2] Be not afraid: the independent artist writing to support her work is pretty different from the student writing to fulfill an assignment.

Students tend to be most familiar with writing assignments in the arts, art history, design, and architecture that ask for critical interpretations of an object, an event, or a structure. Such writing assignments mean analyses informed by history, philosophy, contemporary culture, and so forth. This kind of writing is known as *critical* writing, the standard bearer for academic writing and research. Art educator Linda Apps laments, for instance, that during her student days she "believed that real writing about

DEAR TEACHERS

Please know that this book is intended for you as well as for artists. This guide is my way to share what I've learned from my Professional Practices seminars for students and from my Professional Development workshops with teachers and working artists.

While we know that writing can help students make meaning and integrate knowledge across disciplines, bringing any other considerations into already overloaded curriculums can be a tall order!

The "GuideNotes" section (beginning on page 148) highlights ways to integrate language arts standards and twenty-first-century skills into the arts curriculum. The goal? To help build student confidence with written and visual communication in K–12 and higher education—whatever your particular needs, philosophies of teaching, or resources. The 🔜 symbol will alert you to GuideNotes that correspond to the subject(s) at hand in each chapter:

🔜 **Intro / p.** 148

Thus, these GuideNotes are tied closely to the experiences of art analysis, art making, and art promotion. Please adapt, borrow, or steal from this book at will, and (if you can find the time!) let me know how it all goes.

Sincerely yours,

Kate

art belonged almost explicitly to the domain of critics and theorists."[3] It's clear how students pursuing any major, not just art students, could be intimidated by writing.

Artists Write to Work: A Practical Guide to Writing about Your Art focuses on *applied* writing, the kind of writing that tends to get a bad rap for being generic and uncreative. Think manuals, reports, technical instructions, surveys, encyclopedia entries, letters home to Mom. *Applied* writing may indeed have generic constraints, but it requires a great deal of creativity, knowledge, research, analytical skill, and stamina to bring it into practice. Just think about everything that goes into writing a single email!

EMAIL STANDARDS

Subject Line: The reason for the email itself; a proposition or maybe a question.

Salutation: Formal (Dear [job title, last name]) if recipient is unknown; informal (Dear [first name]) if recipient is known.

Length: Generally two to three brief paragraphs. Since emails transfer communication, attaching longer written documents or images or both is expected.

Request: Any time an "ask," a question about or commitment to something, is being made, try to make the request in the beginning as well as in the end of the email. Suggesting a time frame for the response is a good idea as well.

Closing: Formal (Sincerely, Regards); informal (Best, All the best, etc.).

Reply: Twenty-four hours is the standard response time for emails. If someone doesn't reply after several days, try forwarding the sent email to the recipient with a note: "Dear _____ , I'm resending this email incase the previous one got lost in spam. If you need additional information, please just let me know. I look forward to hearing from you. Sincerely, [your name here]."

Here's what to expect in this practical primer:

Artists Write to Work moves through the stages of the writing and research processes one step at a time. Sections such as "Email FAQs" appear throughout, offering help with standard kinds of communication that artists face every day. Like the "Writing Process into Practice" sections at the end of each chapter, the worksheets that accompany each and every chapter can suggest ways to bring writing process into creative practice.

Chapter 1, "Writing Process || Creative Process," presents the theory behind the parallels between writing and creative processes. It carefully works through how the process of writing relates to the process for an animation production, focusing on the central role an artist's expertise plays.

A NOTE ON NOTES

At the end of each chapter, "Notes" reference scholarship and sources of information. In chapter 1, for instance, the notes reference a wide range of scholarship, including art and design education, writing studies, arts management, art history, literacy studies, communication and marketing, psychology, art criticism, and visual art pedagogy. In later chapters, they're more likely to provide descriptions or share resources. In either event, don't worry! There won't be any tests.

"Doing the Homework," the second chapter, focuses on the artist's mastery and invites her to expand her knowledge about audiences and professional opportunities. Knowledge is, after all, power. This chapter's inverted pyramidal structure moves from research about larger arts institutions to commercial galleries and finally to local arts fairs. Paradoxically, the internet, that global network of information, will be a significant research tool. Readers are encouraged to learn about the art environments that most interest them.

Once the research in chapter 2 is done, it will be time to take stock of accomplishments. Chapter 3, "Taking Inventory," asks readers to do just that: to write down standard personal information (name, rank, and serial number) as well as significant achievements (awards, education, grants, and the like). Having all this content in writing will make it easier to write the Artist Biography and Artist Resume when the time comes.

Chapter 4, "Telling the Story," encourages the reader to engage in more creative and conceptual inventories than those of chapter 3. It asks multiple questions to create multiple perspectives on the art of telling a story, the Artist Statement.

In chapter 5, "Applying Yourself," the artist puts all these processes into practice. The reader has done the research (chapter 2), written the core documents (chapter 3), understood how to tailor the artist statement to given situations (chapter 4), and is prepared to apply himself to a range of opportunities.

"Broadcasting the Word," chapter 6, focuses on strategies for writing promotional materials for announcements and events. In addition to press releases and promotional packets, the chapter explains standards for exhibition wall text.

A singular phrase recurs throughout *Artists Write to Work* and is the title for the concluding chapter: "Only the Individual Artist Can ___": only the individual artist can know, make, plan, choose, visualize, etc. Only the individual artist can know what will fit into her toolbox, and only she can determine which paths to pursue. A last worksheet encourages artists to imagine new audiences, experiences, and opportunities that might be just around the corner.

Finally, case studies in fine art gallery exhibition and public art application complete the volume. They show how to put the research and readings recommended in chapters 2 and 5 into practice.

Some suggestions before turning the page.

This practical primer is built on the premise that independent careers in the arts make demands beyond creative practice. That's a lot of work. Artists, whatever their media, rely on themselves, frequently wearing many hats and learning by trial and error as their careers grow.

Bringing writing process and research into studio practice isn't a clear-cut activity. The fancy French phrase *mise en place*, "everything in its place," seems useful here. Anyone familiar with top-chef television shows probably knows that *mise en place* means getting everything measured, chopped, and placed within easy reach before the baking, cooking, or grilling begins. Bringing writing into daily studio practice requires preparation, and ongoing mindfulness as well.

Here are a few things to have in place:

- Keep a calendar.
- Invite a friend.
- Write it all down.
- Put it into practice.
- Keep smiling

Keep a calendar

Time management can be a real headache. An established calendar can transform initially novel activities (such as writing process) into regular studio practice: write those recurring activities on the calendar.[4]

Invite a friend

Many hands (and minds) make light work. Plus, it makes the work that much more fun. Share this book with a friend. Research (yes! research!) shows that artists crave a community of peers with whom to work.[5] For some, the absence of such a community can be a real hardship, especially for those making the transition from art school to independent careers.

Inviting a friend to work through this guide or any project can be a great way to develop community. Invite some friends by making a bimonthly date (Writing Wednesdays?) to delegate work and to set deadlines, which can help keep the research momentum going.

Write it all down

Don't trust the mind; it can be faulty and fickle. It helps to write it all down.[6]

Writing in journals or small notebooks helps keep track of how ideas develop over time. A catchall file drawer for receipts is always a good idea, too. On the practical side, writing it all down can be a really rewarding record of daily studio practice. Wondering what to document? Everything: dates, times, places, peoples, ideas, inspirations.

Put it into practice

Maintaining studio practice can feel like keeping all the balls in the air for awhile. Maybe even a good long while. It takes skill to bring creative and writing processes into practice, all the while reserving brain and creative space for new projects. Writers write about two to four hours a day; artists who spend at least that much time in their studio report success as well.[7] These excellent habits are established through practice, just like any other skills are developed. The best part? If the best writers write about what they know, it stands to reason that artists, up to their eyeballs in expertise, are the best candidates for writing about their work.

Keep smiling

This book is a primer: a small book on writing for working artists. It's not something to be mastered. There isn't a set timeline; only the individual artist can make and meet his career objectives.

The key is to be excited and to keep momentum about the work. Don't let the doom and gloom of the romantic ideal overshadow the promise of new experiences and opportunities. It's important to enjoy all of the work. Keep smiling![8]

Research, draft, and revise (repeat): these are the writing processes to bring into studio practice. Once everything is in its place, the work on writing can begin. Aspiring, teaching, and working artists who learn about writing on their own often report feeling discouraged, if not downright traumatized. And that's just not right. There's no need to learn how to write the hard way. The objective of this primer? To help readers anxious about or unfamiliar with writing and research bring these processes into studio practice with confidence.

Notes

1. The Bureau of Labor Statistics provides a wealth of statistical information about current employment and forecasts employment for careers in upcoming years.

2. See Halliday's "'I Came to Art School So I Wouldn't Have to Write . . .'" (2005).

3. Apps and Mamchur, "Artful Language" (2009, 270). Artist and researcher Hjelde goes a step further and suggests that a great divide separates formalist education (foundations) and conceptual education (critical thinking and writing) in "Paradox and Potential" (2015, 180). See also Sullivan, "Studio Art as Research Practice" (2004).

4. Battenfield gives great guidance about time management in her *Artist's Guide* (2009).

5. For more about the role that community support plays in art student and independent artist experience, please see Siddins et al., "Building Visual Artists' Resilience Capabilities" (2016); Apps and Mamchur, "Artful Language" (2009); Salazar, "A Portrait of the Artists as Young Adults" (2016); and Welsh et al., "Responding to the Needs and Challenges of Arts Entrepreneurs" (2014).

6. Word processing and spreadsheet software make inserting dates and file names on electronic documents unbelievably easy. Just go to "Insert" and select "Date & Time": mission accomplished.

7. For research on this topic, please see Bridgstock, "Professional Capabilities for Twenty-First Century Creative Careers" (2013) and Toor, "The Habits of Highly Productive Writers" (2014).

8. For more on the science of smiles, see Zajonic et al., "Feeling and Facial Efference" (1989) and Alam et al., "Botulinum Toxin and the Facial Feedback Hypothesis" (2008).

Writing Process || Creative Process

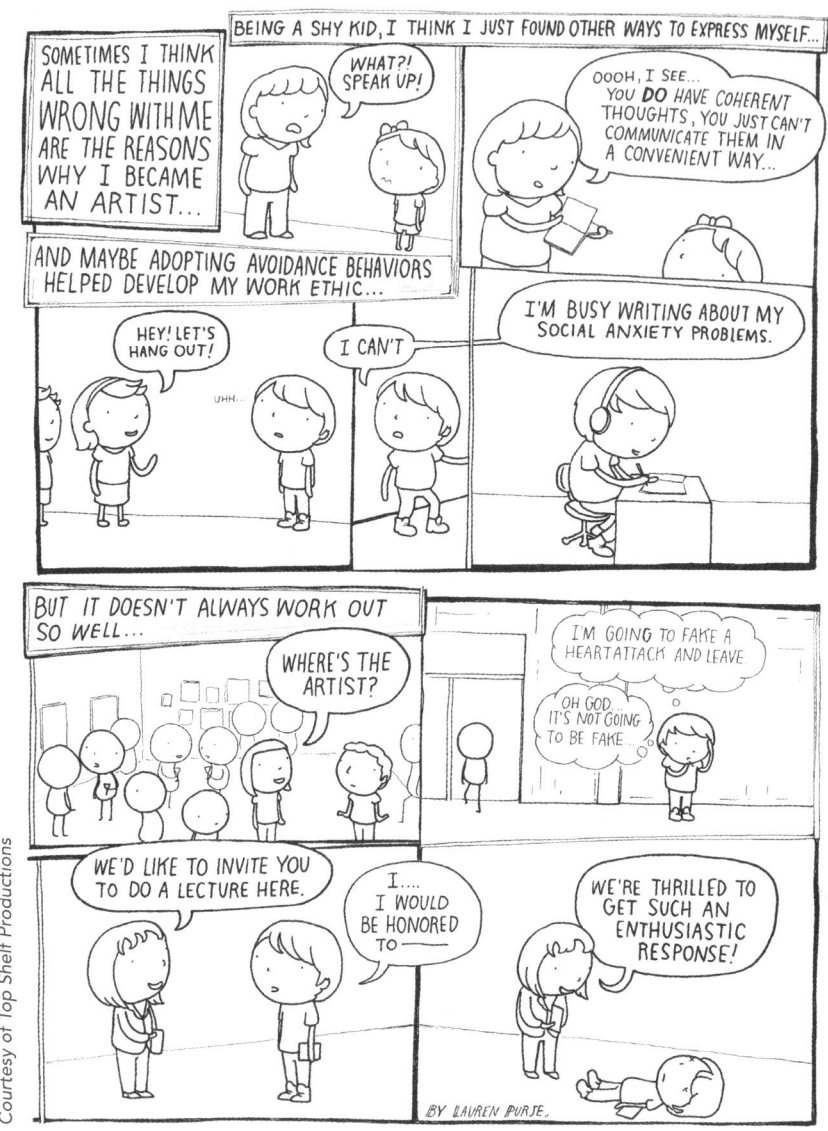

Lauren Purje. *Sometimes I Think All the Things Wrong with Me . . .*,
from *You Might Be an Artist If . . . .* © Lauren Purje, 2017.

Artists can be good, if not great, writers.

REALLY?

Well, yes!

Some artists even use words as media, just like they use paint, clay, metal, found objects, stone, dirt, textiles, wood, video, film, sound, space, and light.[1] This chapter focuses on the similarities between creative and writing processes so that other artists—for whom using words seems as likely as piloting a trip to Mars—can gain confidence and knowledge.[2]

For these less confident writers, memories of well-meaning art appreciators winking about how artists "just think differently" or business folks shrugging about how artists "live in a different world" come to mind pretty quickly. Brooklyn-based artist Lauren Purje addresses all of this in her comic. "Oooh, I see . . .," says the authority figure. "You DO have coherent thoughts, you just can't communicate them in a convenient way." Purje's comic pokes fun, but that poke smarts, too.

Dismissive attitudes are all too familiar (and harmful) to working artists, especially to those in the beginning of their careers.[3] Purje's fictional student seeks comfort in "writing about my social anxiety problems," a defensive action that can lead to a strong work ethic, one that happens to include writing, in this instance.

Research suggests that Purje's fictional student is indeed really on to something, that confiding in a journal is a good way to work through anxiety, to be productive.[4] Those who find such a practice helpful are encouraged to do so!

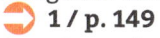 **1 / p. 149**

Creative and studio artists' learning styles are frequently understood as visual, spatial, experiential, subjective, and kinetic. Such characterizations neglect the objective, logical, or linear reasoning involved in creative processes. To engage different kinds of learners across the spectrum, for instance, this practical primer presents information textually (prose), graphically (bulleted and numbered lists), visually (images and text boxes), and actively (worksheets).

Art teachers lament the great divide between making art and writing, which becomes wider during elementary school. By the time kids get to high school, the division seems to be set in stone. Many artists won't believe they are good at writing (think critical essays), while many writers won't believe they are good at art (think representational drawings). It's understandable that some artists express anxiety about writing: they just don't have much experience with it.[5]

When writing instruction does happen, it seems like it's outside of creative processes. A vicious cycle can come into play: studio art faculty complain that incoming students don't know how to write, and students wonder why the faculty expect them to know how to do so! As Linda Apps puts it, "Historically there seems to be a tacit understanding upheld by instructors and [art] students alike, that writing is marginal, in addition to the art."[6]

Exceptions exist, of course, such as the critical-writing sequence offered at the University of the Arts (Philadelphia, Pennsylvania) or the occasional writing seminars at other institutions.[7] Such writing instruction is noteworthy for exploring how the role of critical reading and writing relates to the practice of making. Some institutions, such as the University of Minnesota, require intensive writing components in all courses, in all disciplines. Unlike the exceptional training in creative processes in the fine, applied, and performing arts, training in the writing process itself tends to be fairly rare in formal arts education in the US.[8]

AFTER SCHOOL

Writing education for artists comes into play after school, both literally and figuratively. Evening and weekend courses and workshops regularly occur through continuing education programs at art departments and art academies. Community art centers, member arts organizations, and maker conferences frequently host hands-on workshops for professional development as well. Business-of-art or professional-practices workshops are great places to keep honing writing skills.

Many art students working on doctorates (PhDs), such as the students in a study by Australian sociologist Jacquelyn Allen Collinson, report that they just didn't have that much experience with writing, that their undergraduate and graduate educations emphasized "communication via making, with little attention to written communication."[9] Given the relative absence of writing instruction, it's not too surprising that the students in this study reported "some shock [to] the new domain of research" that required them to communicate in writing as well.[10]

Later, these students commented on "a positive change in the use of their hands. Previously, the focus of their hands had been with the making; now their hands were capable of working at a sophisticated level in another dimension."[11] The physical contact between pen and paper led these students to another creative dimension—an appreciation for the writing process: Writing as reflection. Writing as documentation. Writing as communication. Writing as reasoning. And, for artists, writing as "a positive change in the use of their hands."[12]

WRITING TO SEE

There are many teachers who inventively try to reduce the gap between the artist/writer divide. In *Syllabus: Notes from an Accidental Professor*, for instance, Lynda Barry encourages her students to "write what [they] see."[13] These University of Wisconsin–Madison undergrads are neither artists nor writers, but they all draw, write, and theorize creativity.

> To get an A, you must not only spend more time on assignments and demonstrate active engagement with the work, you must also find something original during the course of the semester.
>
> What I mean by "finding something original" may be hard to define on paper, but it's unmistakable when it starts to happen. . . . A new way of seeing comes about, a new approach to problem-solving and working that extends beyond the limits of our class time into other aspects of daily life.[14]

The text of Barry's *Syllabus* is a work of art in and of itself: a composition book filled with syllabi, drawings, writings, and a host of silly and sophisticated paraphernalia.

Process

Here's the thing: artists are the very best people to write about their work. Why? Because artists know the most about their work. This seems pretty straightforward. Artists are fluent in formal standards such as composition, color, line, texture, scale, symmetry, and contrast, as well as methods and techniques.

Unlike those who write *about* art, artists are steeped in formal and stylistic knowledge.[15] Artists know more about themselves, their practice, and their processes than anyone else in the whole world. The real question is why artists would let anyone else write for them!

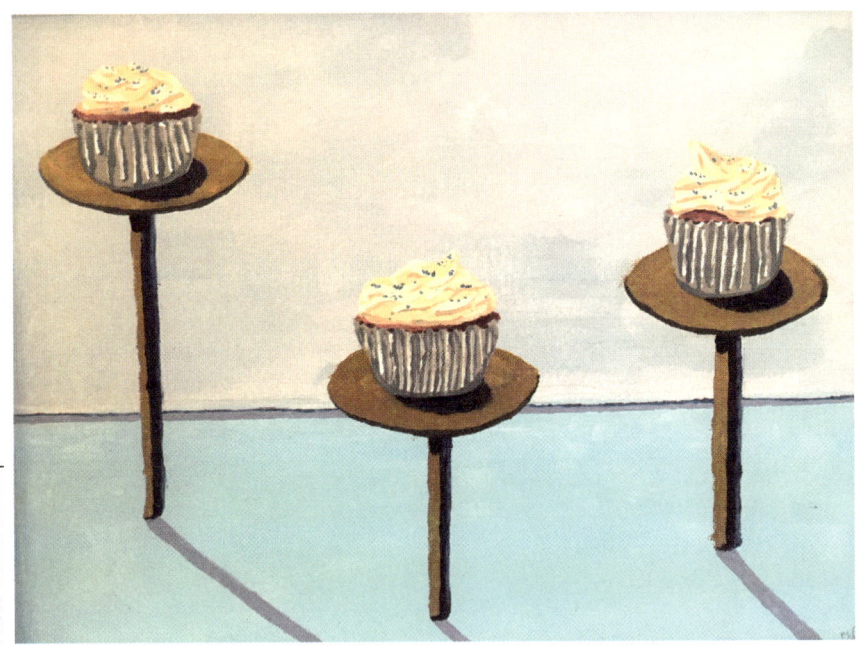

Charlotte Poehlmann. *Cupcakes à la Thibaud*, 2017.
Acrylic on canvas.

Every artist makes decisions about her work, prepares for the work, and then does the work. The painter who decides to make an acrylic painting, for instance, goes through many stages. First, the artist prepares the canvas:

- Build a frame
- Measure canvas
- Cut canvas

- Stretch canvas
- Prime and gesso canvas

The diligent artist might even gesso the canvas twice.

Then the artist begins the creative process. Artist Charlotte Poehlmann outlined this series of steps for the *Cupcakes à la Thibaud* acrylic painting:

- Sketch out composition
- Paint background
  top half
  bottom half
- Draw cake holders
- Mix colors
- Paint cake holders
- Let it dry
- Draw cupcakes on cake holders
- Mix colors
  gray
  dark gray
  light gray
- Paint cupcake holders
- Let it dry
- Draw icing

- Mix colors
  cream
  dark cream
  light cream
- Paint icing
- Let it dry
- Mix colors
- Paint red velvet cupcake
- Let it dry
- Draw shadows
- Mix colors
- Paint shadows
- Let it dry
- Paint highlights and sprinkles

For artists, these steps are old news. Many readers are no doubt nodding their heads, saying "Yes, yes . . . of course." It might all be familiar to you, dear reader, but for nonspecialists, artists work magic.

The above shows, I hope, that it's important to explain, or at least to keep in mind, the novelty of these foundational basics and methods to non-artists. Knowledge about art history and theory acquired over the course of demanding art programs are also significant. It's important to talk about how to bring these highly specialized ways of thinking about creative process into clear view, into something that can then be communicated in writing. The editors of *Draw it with your eyes closed* identify this conscious knowledge as "a creative response to an ever-changing set of external demands."[16]

The independent artist communicates all of this discipline and insight to the rest of us through their work and in writing. The good news: the writing process runs parallel to creative process. Time is a friend both to artist and writer. Note how the time, the "let it dry" resting spots between the steps for the acrylic painting process, allows things to settle.

In this next section, a standard art assignment will serve as a case study. It will help demonstrate just how aligned creative and writing processes can be.

The VisualPoetic [sic] assignment, which my former colleague Mat Rappaport (Columbia College, Chicago) provided, calls for a twenty-second motion graphics animation.[17] The assignment recommends that a fragment from a text, such as something from a poem or from an overheard conversation, could serve as the inspiration for the project. Here's the assignment's Objective:

The intent of the project is to allow you to create a motion graphics animation in which you can apply and refine design, animation and transition principles, while exploring a more open[-]ended subject.

Sounds fun! Students are asked to demonstrate their mastery and understanding of design, animation, and transition principles and to choose their own content.

The assignment then provides a Rubric:

For full credit you must complete all components of the project on time. The final animation must be no longer than 20 seconds, include a combination of graphic elements, typography, pattern and color scheme [in motion]. The animation must evoke the underlying meaning/s of the text while maintaining an overall aesthetic cohesion.

It is advisable to develop a structure which employs repetition or theme and variation. Examples of this may include having the first and last phrase reference one another [bookends] in visual theme, optical camera effects or motion.

Sounds hard! The final product needs all the visuals, text, sound, and motion to work together in a cohesive, logical whole. The "structure" that organizes all these elements is central to the project's success.

Finally, the assignment provides a useful blueprint in the Process section (emphases in italics added below):

- Proposal (a one-page *written* interpretation of the chosen text's meaning)

- Visual discovery/research (multiple samples that "[are] your collection of inspirations" and mood boards "to create a visual system that helps you discover the *internal visual logic* of the text")

- Style frames that are radically different approaches to the content ("Think about materials or *visual subcultures* as a way of differentiating the compositions")

- Storyboards ("to *describe* the major compositions and the *transitions*")

- Audio composition ("must have some rhythmic *structure* but does not need to be musical")

- Keyframes ("a finished keyframe for each of the *major* compositions in your storyboard")

- Test animations ("produce a set of tests which show *multiple* solutions to one of the phrases and one of the *transitions*")

- Final animation

The processes in this assignment are sophisticated. The students are asked to write a proposition, brainstorm the project's internal logic, outline possible perspectives, describe major ideas and the transitions between them, organize the material into a logical structure, craft blocks of material, draft a few possibilities, and polish a final artifact.

Likewise, writers work to craft clear and concise propositions that engage reasoning just like the "Style Frames" section does. Proposition (what is the purpose?), Plan (how can the material be presented or organized? in what sequence?), Audience (to whom will the work appeal?),and Goal (what change or impact does the artist/writer want to achieve?). Much like the students engaging in the VisualPoetic assignment, writers might craft pre-outlines to identify key reasons and evidence. Both artists and writers typically engage in some form of peer review or critique to see if the project makes sense as well. If room for improvement exists, artists and writers can always go back to the drawing board and revise.

A side-by-side comparison of the creative and the writing processes looks something like the table on the facing page, "Motion Graphics Animation Process || Writing Process." As the table demonstrates, the vocabulary for the creative and writing processes might be specialized, but the processes run parallel to one another. Both artists and writers propose, brainstorm, research, outline, draft, organize, complete draft, give feedback, and finalize draft.

Ready to take on the writing process? Move on to the Writing Process || Creative Process Taking Stock Worksheet (p. 118), which promotes self-awareness about an artist's creative and writing processes. Find the worksheet too formal? Writing in a journal might be more fun. The goal remains the same: the artist who's more self-aware about the who, what, when, where, and how of creative processes is better equipped to communicate in writing.

Motion Graphics Animation Process	Writing Process
Written purpose, methods, strategies, objectives	Written purpose, methods, strategies, objectives
Proposal	Proposal
Brainstorming	Brainstorming
Visual Discovery Research online, in the field, in the library	Research online, in the field, in the library
Research	Research
Pre-outlining	Pre-outlining
Style Frames	Organizing blocks of visual and written reasoning
Organizing blocks of visual and audio reasoning	Drafts
Storyboard	Strengthening transitions between blocks of reasoning
Explaining transitions between blocks of reasoning	Revisions
Audio Composition + Key Frames	
Testing reasoning structure	Testing reasoning structure
Test Animations	Peer Reviews
Final Draft	Final Draft

Practice

Practice, as a concept, is broad in scope. It describes how artists get used to methods and processes in their daily work, their daily practice. Some might keep regular studio hours, while others might engage in practice around the clock.[18]

For artist Mary Heilmann (American, b. 1940), for instance, work and life are one and the same: "All of my time is work time, and all of my work time is made out of my free time. In a rather obsessive-compulsive way, I am constantly spinning thoughts around my head, thinking of work that I might create."[19]

And Heilmann engages in quite a lot of work:

Teaching, and the thoughts and conversations, connections, and friendships that came with teaching and its relationship to the community of the art world . . . combined with my free time to give me the substance, the concepts, the skills, that it took for me to produce paintings, sculptures, pots, tiles, etchings, silk screens, videos, photographs, chairs, tables, fabric, lamps, everything I make with my hand with the help of many assistants, printmakers, cabinetmakers, camera operators, and even sound mixers. So free time, work time—it's all of a piece.[20]

Heilmann concludes with the phrase "it's all of a piece," all of the lived experience and creative processes are pieces of the seamless whole. In an episode of *Art:21* on PBS (2009), she talks about how writing for such magazines as *Art Journal* is central to her thinking and hence to her work; how writing titles for her works of art is like crafting three-word poems.[21]

These passages shed light on how writing and research can add to studio practice 24/7: "subject area" and "free time" can happen all at once. It's all of a piece. Only an individual artist can know how and when to bring these processes into practice.

Writing Process into Practice

Interested in bringing writing process into studio practice? Here are some things to consider:

1. Knowledge

   Knowledge with a capital "K" rules, every single time. Knowledge about art methods, concepts, media, and process, as well as art history, culture, literature, life, land, politics, and social justice. The working artist knows more about her art than anyone else. She'll also know which documents will support her applications and exhibitions best.

2. Preparation

   Having everything in place, such as the right supplies, helps save time and expense when preparing for a project. This includes keeping a journal at the ready. It also includes learning more about opportunities and those who offer them.

3. Drafts

   Sketching can bring enough confidence to take risks, making room for happy, unexpected accidents. Likewise, brainstorming ideas in writing can lead to surprising results.

4. Final Steps

   Polishing the final work. An artwork might need to be sprayed with a fixative or waxed to preserve it. A written document will need to be stored in a safe place or saved to a computer or jump drive.

The artist's writing process follows a similar trajectory, start to finish.

1. Knowledge

   Knowing what documents will be required for an activity or an application and to whom the documents will be addressed.

2. Preparation

   Researching potential audiences is a general given to achieve effective written communication. The writing artist knows how much to explain and what vocabulary words will be most useful.

3. Drafts

Writing drafts of the required documents provides time to revise, to modify as deadlines draw near.

4. Final Steps

Revising final materials for polish and then sending them on their way.

Not-so-subtle reminder: getting everything into place can help bring writing process and research into studio practice. Invite a friend. Keep a calendar. Write it down. Put it into practice. Keep smiling.

Notes

1. Late-twentieth-century American contemporary artists Jenny Holzer, Bruce Nauman, and Mark Tansey rank among the usual suspects who use words as media. Still others are renowned for their role as art critics, too, such as the reviews by minimalist Donald Judd in the early 1960s, critical essays by conceptualist artist Robert Morris during the same time period, and critiques by contemporary artist Barbara Kruger more recently.

2. Apps and Mamchur, "Artful Language" (2009) and Andrelchik, "Reconsidering Literacy in the Art Classroom" (2015) also address how writing process and creative process need to be integrated into rather than polarized in art education.

3. Hemmig discusses this issue at length in "The Information-Seeking Behavior of Visual Artists" (2008).

4. See Mueller and Oppenheimer, "The Pen Is Mightier Than the Keyboard" (2014) and Nguyen, "10 Surprising Benefits You'll Get from Keeping a Journal" (2015).

5. Ruby Lerner, founding president and executive director of Creative Capital, identifies a number of other considerations she'd like to see, in "The Art School of the Future": "art theory, practice and technical training with a professional development curriculum ... strategic planning, goal setting, work/life balance, and time management. ... And ... a LOT of time on communications—verbal communications, presentation skills, negotiating, marketing, outreach and PR" (57).

6. Apps and Mamchur, "Artful Language" (2009, 270).

7. Maryland Institute College of Art's Joseph Meyerhoff Center for Career Development is another example of a program that focuses on professional development (www. mica.edu).

8. See Johnson et al., "The Use of Writing in the Apparel Curriculum: A Preliminary Investigation" (2003).

9. Collinson, "Artistry and Analysis: Student Experiences of UK Practice-Based Doctorates in Art and Design" (2005, 722).

10. Ibid., 717.

11. Ibid., 722.

12. Ibid., 722.

13. Barry, *Syllabus* (2015, 1).

14. Ibid., 59.

15. Many excellent resources on the market address credible, effective, and persuasive art historical analysis. See, for instance, Barnet, *A Short Guide to Writing about Art* (2011) and D'Alleva, *Look! The Fundamentals of Art History* (2004).

16. *Paper Monument* (2012, 122).

17. All citations from Rappaport's "Project 3: VisualPoetic" Motion Graphics I assignment (2013).

18. See Robinson, "Underwriting: An Experience in Charting Studio Practice" (2009).

19. Heilmann, "Obsessive-Compulsive Daydreaming" (2011), 43.

20. Ibid., 49.

21. Heilmann, https://art21.org/artist/mary-heilmann/.

Doing the Homework

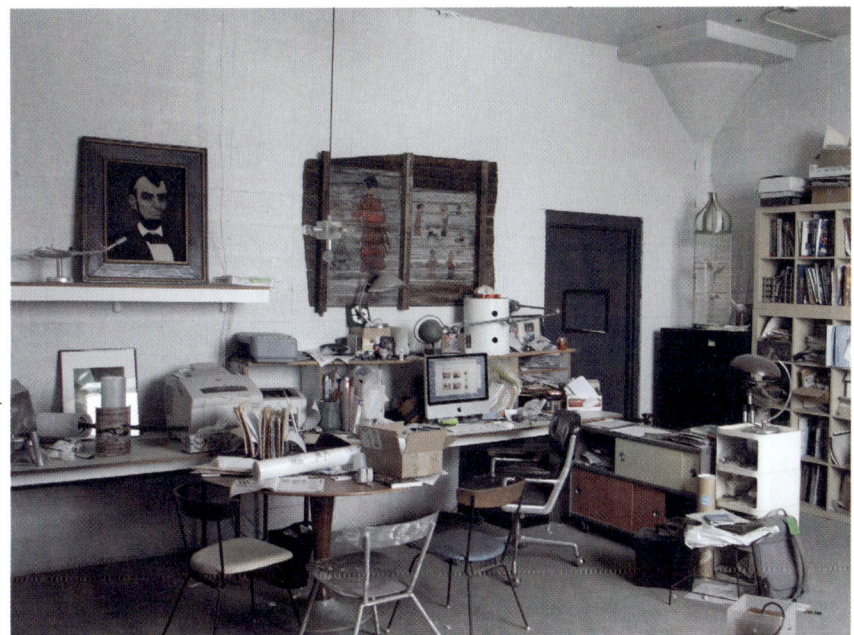

Photo credit © 2010 Christopher Poehlmann

Sculptor studio office.

One hopes that after reading through chapter 1 and working through the Taking Stock Worksheet (p. 118), how to bring the writing process into studio practice seems less daunting, maybe even welcome.

The next hurdle: learn more about the wide varieties of audiences in the arts. This hurdle isn't very high, but it does require time and effort. The best research tools—those necessary instruments familiar both to artists and writers—will be internet access and something to write with. If a friend has yet to be invited to work on a particular project, today might be the day to do so.

Whether working solo or with a team, the step-by-step research strategy follows general guidelines: please improvise at will. Forecasting (and then meeting) deadlines on the calendar might be a really great way to keep the research moving forward. If nothing else, those deadlines will be gentle reminders to resume research.

AUDIENCE

Note that the reference to "audience" as opposed to "market" is purposeful. *Artists Write to Work* envisions a reader who wants to make a living from her art and to gain recognition for her career. This reader might identify herself as a self-employed independent contractor—someone wanting to make a living from her work. Others might be more entrepreneurial, interested in making money (via production and distribution) by marketing someone else's work.

In either case, *audience* is the preferred term in this primer because it is flexible, referencing commercial as well as educational, nonprofit, and other fine art communities.

This chapter takes on local research first. Do proceed with patience: this research is a process! Along the way, the arts community will expand to include more artists and arts enthusiasts.

Local + Regional Art Organizations

Local and regional arts groups can be found nearly everywhere. Learning more about the roles these institutions play can be incredibly useful. Sometimes this information is developed organically, particularly when a region has been home to an artist for a long time. Doing the homework can help such an artist organize the material and maybe even track career trajectories. For those new to an area, doing the homework is a great way to become familiar with what a region has to offer.

There's no better place to start than the artist's backyard.

⮕ **2 / p. 150**

Focus on information about nonprofit art institutions, local or regional nonprofit art organizations, community arts centers, academic galleries, and museums to make the research worthwhile. Interested in getting a work donated to an institution? Focus on collecting organizations. More interested in exhibition opportunities? Focus on exhibiting organizations. Interested in both opportunities? Just write it all down. What seems obvious on the day of a gallery visit can too quickly become a distant memory.

⮕ **2.1 / p. 150**

Here's a quick overview of different kinds of nonprofit arts organizations:

1. Nonprofit Collecting Art Museums

Museums conserve and often present a wide range of art and artifacts. Artists in the immediate vicinity can feel excluded or neglected by such institutions, but familiarity with the overall missions of such institutions will shed light on an individual museum's culture and its willingness to exhibit work by contemporary artists.

Individual museums may not present or collect contemporary art, but they may host volunteer or donor committees, groups, or both that are interested in particular media. Check them out! Maybe even join a committee.

For those who are outgoing and sociable, after-hours events and exhibition openings are great places to meet museum professionals, other artists, and art appreciators.

2. Local or Regional Nonprofit Art Organizations

Missions of these organizations range from supporting completely historical to exclusively contemporary art. These nonprofits can be extraordinarily supportive of emerging artists, providing opportunities for exhibitions as well as resources such as continuing education.

Like larger institutions, these organizations have a variety of initiatives. Explore their websites to determine key people, activities, and opportunities to participate.

3. Community Arts Centers

These centers sometimes offer workshops, lectures, studio space, and other resources to their members. Some may even have regular children or teen programming available. Gallery exhibitions may feature work of members as well as invitational or juried exhibitions.

See #2 above, second item.

4. Academic Galleries and Museums

Some of these institutions are bare bones—mounting student art exhibitions twice a year—while others host programming that is world renowned. The only way to find out about them is to visit them, their websites, or both.

If an institution happens to be your alma mater, let them know your insider status. Working with the powers that be can be a worthwhile endeavor indeed.

See #2 above, second item.

Where, one might ask, does this information live? On an organization's website, of course. These websites are gold mines of information about arts professionals, collectors, donors, committees, institutional initiatives, and so forth. Look for the About Us, FAQs, Staff, Join & Support, Friends, and Board of Directors tabs on the websites.

Keep an eye out for information that might include any of the following:

- Mission

- Major collections

- Major exhibitions

- Exhibition opportunities

- Themes / genres

- Key employees (directors, curators, et al.)

- Sponsors

- Committees or support groups

- Affiliations

- Education

Then write that information down.

Good looks at organizations will show which institutions will be most relevant to a developing career (see Arts Organizations Worksheet, p. 122).

A spreadsheet to begin recording arts organizations in the Philadelphia and Delaware River Valley region might look something like this:[1]

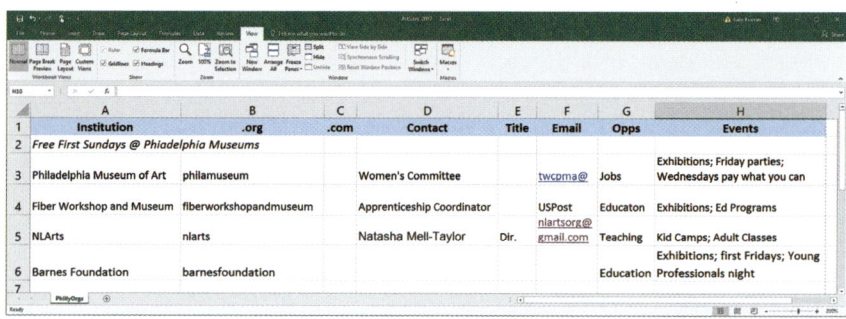

KEY

Institution: Name of Institution
.org: nonprofit website
.com: commercial website
Contact: name of contact

Title: title of contact
Email: email address
Opps: exhibition or work opportunities
Events: public events

This Artsites_2017 workbook in Microsoft Excel is pretty straightforward. The lower-left tab, PhillyOrgs, identifies its subject matter by its spreadsheet name.[2] Spreadsheets are visually accessible, readily adaptable, and easily searchable as the research process continues. In this practical primer, additional spreadsheets will be added to the Artsites_2017 workbook.

A million other ways to categorize and capture the data do, of course, exist. Only the individual artist can know what methods and terms work best for him.

The most important thing is to write it all down. Research can be organized by type of organization, by media, and by location. But write it down. Write it as narrative, in a spreadsheet, as notes, etc. But write it down to bring it all into practice. Getting to know the roles that various institutions and staff members play helps bring potential audiences into focus.

SHARE THE WORK

Thought about whom to invite yet? Sharing the work can help speed up the process and make it all that much more rewarding. One artist can work on the collecting institutions, their support groups such as the Philadelphia Museum of Art's Women's Group, social and educational events, and job opportunities, while the other artist can focus on contemporary arts museums or centers, their support groups, etc. Being a working artist means being part of the art scene (by going to events of interest) as well as continuing to learn (by seeing as much art as possible).

Local + Regional Commercial Art Galleries

Researching art galleries might be the best way to find out which galleries might be the best possibilities for future representation. And it's fun, too: regularly visit galleries at their brick-and-mortar locations, talk with peers about their experiences with galleries, and keep an eye on the tabloids. That Dream Gallery everyone raves about might be a nightmare, troubled by unhappy (read: unpaid) artists or legal issues. During gallery visits, artists are interviewing the galleries as much as the galleries are getting to know new and emerging artists.

Fine craft. Fine art. Handmade. Installation. Decorative art. Sculpture. These generic terms mean something in the art and commercial worlds. Abstract. Realist. Multimedia. American. They have many subgenres, and their borders blend.

Knowing as much as one can might mean getting a foot in the door (of an enviable contemporary art gallery) rather than putting a foot in the mouth (by submitting a portfolio of ceramic vessels to an abstract art gallery).

Getting out into the field will be even more enjoyable if a friend is invited along! Those new to an area will meet many like-minded people at these events, while long-term residents will have fun with their tried-and-true crowd. In addition to keeping track of events and hosting institutions, include the organizers, other participants, and new contacts. After all, the art world is a pretty small place when it comes right down to it. One never knows how or through whom networks expand!

First impressions can mean everything. Doing the Homework: Commercial Art Galleries Worksheet (see p. 124) formalizes these first impressions. It asks for written accounts about the gallery environment, the installation design itself, the career levels of the artists on display, and the featured artists.

GALLERY EVENTS

Write it on the calendar; invite friends! Visiting galleries is a great way to meet other artists as well as arts professionals. Enjoy the free appetizers and beverages as well as the free exposure to a wide variety of people interested in the arts: it's all part of community building.

This worksheet, like the others, is adaptable: prioritize as needed! The goal: to learn enough about the local opportunities to know which places will be the best fit. How welcoming is the staff? What's the price of the art? What's the range of expertise? Who's in charge? Write careful notes about first impressions as well as reflections. Knowing price ranges according to career status (new, emerging, midcareer), media, and subject matter within a region can take some of the guesswork out of pricing. Finding a home for the art may be the ultimate goal, but it's important to have fun along the way.

Want to formalize the local gallery survey even further? A spreadsheet exploring the art scene in the Twin Cities area of Minneapolis / St. Paul, Minnesota, might start out looking like this:

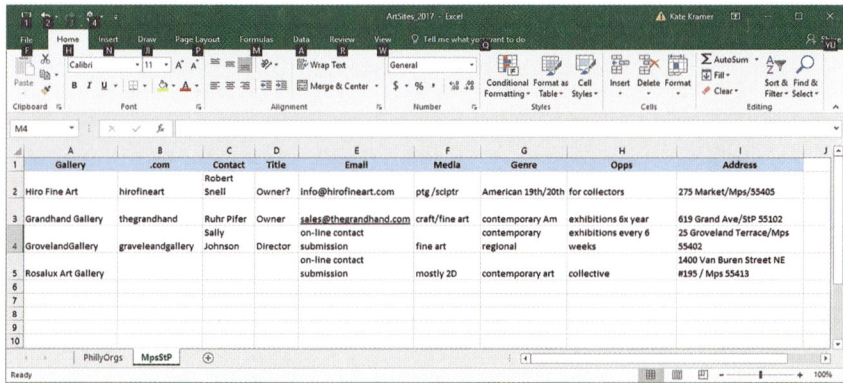

The brief survey in the MpsStp spreadsheet yielded some valuable intel: the Grand Hand Gallery website let artists know that it encourages interested artists to get in touch, to get involved even though it wasn't reviewing unsolicited portfolios at the moment.[3] Similar opportunities and suggestions were given on the Rosalux Art Gallery website.

To live in the greater Minneapolis / St. Paul metropolitan area would mean exploring new and established galleries, online as well as at their brick-and-mortar locations, to find out what's going on. For the research itself, writing it all down is the thing to do.

Like the PhillyOrgs spreadsheet, if the Mps_St.P spreadsheet appeals, use it! If it doesn't, just get to work researching and write the information in a different format.

Local + Regional Art Fairs

Beyond arts centers, museums, galleries, and collectives, another whole realm of art representation exists: the art fair. The more local the fair, the more regularly the event is held outside under tents; the more professional the fair, the more often the event is held indoors at distinct sites such as Navy Piers (Sculpture Objects Functional Art and Design [SOFA] in Chicago) and freestanding buildings (Frieze in New York City) or convention centers (Art Basel in Miami, Florida).

Indeed, geography might be the best way to define and explore these opportunities. Like nonprofit arts organizations, there are many different kinds of arts fairs.

1. Street Fairs

These are typically organized by local municipalities, business or community organizations, or even small businesses specializing in local arts and crafts.

Fees for participation are relatively low (under $100), but the exhibitor usually needs to provide his own booth.

For the student or emerging artist, these can be good ways to practice showcasing and talking about her own work.

2. Regional Fairs and Art Festivals

There are many working artists who "work the circuit" all year long: exhibiting work in the South and West in the winters; focusing on the Midwest, Northeast, and Northwest in the summers; returning to their home studios to create new inventories for the upcoming cycle of fairs; then going back out on the road. Similar seasonal cycles exist on the West Coast as well.

Many an artist applies to specific fairs in his region to take advantage of the art-appreciating audiences sure to visit the fair.

Submissions typically go through a jury review process.

Fees for participation are higher ($300 and up).

The exhibitor always needs to provide her own booth.

Callsforartists.com and callforentry.org are excellent sources for opportunities across the United States.

3. Fine Art and Craft Fairs / Individual

These tend to be targeted toward more-specialized audiences, those predisposed to fine art and craft.

American Craft Council shows are a good barometer nationwide (see www.craftcouncil.org/shows).

Submissions go through jury review process.

Fees for participation are higher ($1,000 and up).

The exhibitor always needs to provide his own booth.

Some fairs are hosted by regional fine art organizations.

Callsforartists.com is an excellent source for opportunities across the United States.

4. Fine Art, Craft, and Furniture Fairs / Commercial

Like individual fine art and craft fairs, these tend to be targeted toward more specialized audiences, those predisposed to fine art and craft.

Unlike individual fine art and craft fairs, galleries or other consortia are responsible for all application processes, fees, and staffing.

A particular gallery might bring every artist it represents, or just a few such as SOFA (Sculptural Objects Functional Art and Design) in Chicago and Frieze in New York City.

5. Blue Chip Contemporary Art Fairs

International in scope, these fairs are targeted toward highly specialized audiences.

Blue chip galleries from around the world travel around the world to exhibit at these fairs.

Like fine art, craft, and furniture fairs, these galleries or other consortia are responsible for all application processes, fees, and staffing.

Notable fairs include Art Basel in Miami and EXPO in Chicago.

6. Satellite Contemporary Art Installations

International in scope, these installations take place on the periphery of blue chip contemporary art fairs, sometimes in hotels, on streets, or even in shipping containers.

They are typically organized collaboratively by particularly entrepreneurial artist or arts enthusiasts or sometimes by a local arts organization.

Applications, fees, and staffing all fall to those who are participating.

How to find them? Visit the blue chip fairs, explore, and make connections. Many of the satellite installations occur organically due to local artist interest and tend to be one-time-only kinds of events.

MAJOR FINE ART + CRAFT FAIRS, USA

JAN (early) FOG Art + Design, San Francisco

(late) ART, Los Angeles

FEB (mid-) ART, Palm Springs

(mid-/late) ACC, Baltimore

MAR (early) ACC, Atlanta

(mid-) Armory Show, NYC

APR (early) ACC, St. Paul

(mid-) Dallas Art Fair

MAY (early) Frieze, NYC

(early) Armory Show, NYC

(mid-) Design Week, NYC

(late) Martha's Vineyard Fair

JUN

JUL (mid-) Art Santa Fe

AUG (early) ACC, Santa Fe

SEP (mid-) startup LA

OCT (late) ART Toronto

(late) Texas Contemporary, Houston

NOV (early/mid-) SOFA, Chicago

DEC (early) Art Basel, Miami

Why do artists and gallerists participate in any of these time-consuming, energy-draining commercial events? To make sales, of course; but also to promote themselves or those they represent, to gain exposure to wider audiences, to engage or reconnect with like-minded arts enthusiasts, to keep current with contemporary fine art and craft, and ultimately to gain credibility and name recognition.

CALENDAR

The art world is full of things to do, and it's easy to get overwhelmed. In part, developing and maintaining a regular schedule is part of establishing a successful studio practice. Things to keep on the calendar might include:

- deadlines
- openings
- art events

- lectures
- workshops
- goals

A regular schedule also makes it easy to make room for unplanned events.[4]

A number of websites share information about art fairs open to independent artists.[5] To find out about specific fairs such as the American Craft Council (ACC) shows, subscribe to major arts magazines and listservs. Membership in specific organizations—by media or professional association—is a great way to receive information about upcoming opportunities as well. Doing the homework can build confidence and help identify logical (as well as profitable and supportive) arts communities and spaces.

THE BACKSTORY

Want to find out more about particular exhibitions? Galleries? Key figures? Check out articles in newspapers and magazines online. Type in a search term such as the title of the event and the gallery. If you're using Google, hit the "Press" tab—it's right there next to the "Images" tab—and a number of articles and reviews should appear. Unlike the listed articles and press releases that an event or organization posts to a "Press" or "News" category on its website, the articles in the greater media will be more objective.

Writing Process into Practice

For the new working artist, the world of information introduced in this chapter might be completely uncharted territory and might seem really difficult to navigate. For the seasoned artists, it is hoped that this material reminds them of the amazing amount of knowledge they have about their art communities and audiences.

Like any other trip, it's important to decide where to begin.

The art student or emerging artist, for example, might start on the street level at the fairs and at the galleries. Or maybe he belongs to an organization, school, or program that sponsors booths at select exhibitions. In any case, showing in a few select shows might take an artist into new neighborhoods in larger metropolitan areas or into new cities in certain regions.

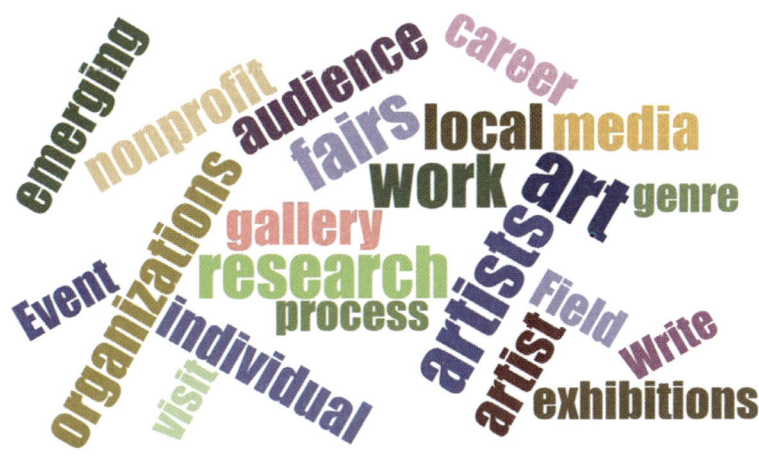

Destinations

It's impossible to attend every single art exhibition or event. So, write down some itineraries for particular dates and invite a copilot who is open to detours all along the way.

Explorations

Interested in traveling up the road to blue chip contemporary art? The itinerary might become international in scope. High-end contemporary art events can be excellent opportunities to rendezvous with like travelers. Not fortunate enough to have work displayed at these fairs? Exploring and making return-trip plans—maybe even underwritten trips by sponsoring galleries—to satellite exhibitions could make their way onto upcoming itineraries.

Write it all down.

Whatever the itinerary, it can't be repeated enough: regular visits to key spots are important elements in every artist's regular practice. Thankfully, the voyage doesn't happen in a day, but over the course of a career. The recorded details can serve as touchstones in a conversation or a letter of inquiry: "When I visited your gallery in October, the inviting atmosphere was really impressive, especially since some visitors might find the art in the main gallery really challenging." When a writer references an actual space, she demonstrates that the artist has done her homework and has thought about how a working relationship might be mutually beneficial. A little bit of knowledge can go a long way.

Notes

1. Welcome to Office Help & Training (https://support.office.com/en-us) is a good resource for tutorials on Excel spreadsheets.

2. Spreadsheets are also really great ways to archive work produced, exhibited, and sold. Please see Bhandari and Melber's *Art/Work* (2009).

3. Information for Artists (http://thegrandhand.com/about/information-for-artists/)

4. Smith and Viders's *Art Office* (2007) might not be as visually appealing as some other business-of-art books, but it features easy-to-use or modified forms. Its subtitle says it all: *80+ Business Forms, Charts, Sample Letters, Legal Documents & Business Plans for Fine Artists*. Most significantly, it has a number of calendar options to help artists establish routines and to keep track of activities on a daily, weekly, monthly, quarterly, and annual basis.

5. For a complete list of internet resources referenced in this book, please see "Internet Resources" (p. 106).

Taking Inventory:
The Artist Resume and Artist Biography

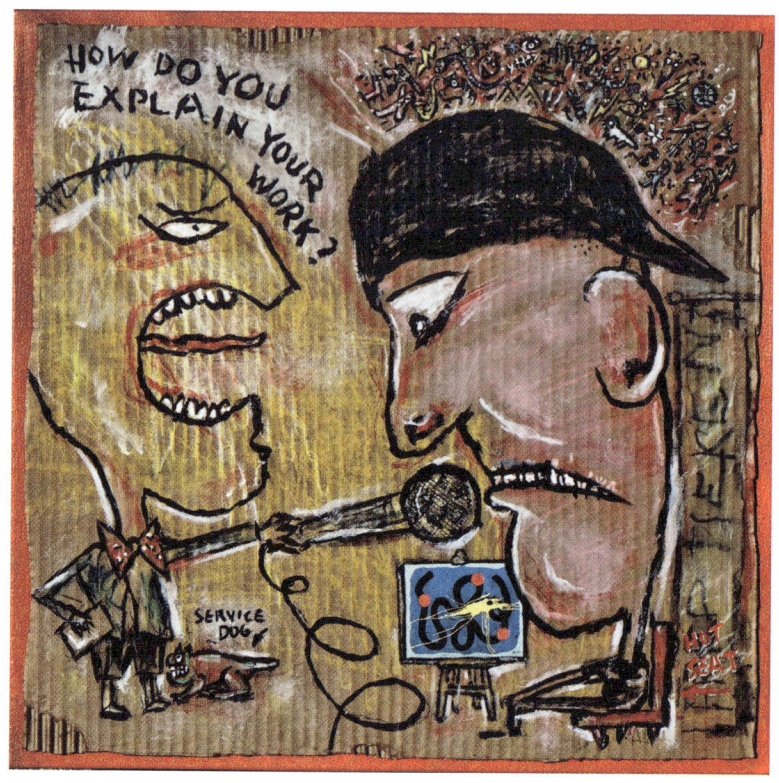

Fred Tieken, 2017. *Artist Statement.*
Acrylic on cardboard and canvas. © *Fred Tieken, 2017*

If the artist learns a lot about local art communities in chapter 2, chapter 3 turns the tables by providing ways for him to school those art communities with the Artist Resume and Artist Biography. Those who are able to write their own documents will communicate their own vision better than anyone else.

A student once asked, "Won't my galleries write these documents? Isn't that their job?" The answer? They'd probably rather not. True, good galleries or artist representatives might take care of their artists' business and promotional responsibilities.[1]

However, for artists working without such responsible representation, the mother lode of the daily writing and promotional work will fall on their shoulders. No matter how good the representation, though, it's up to the artists to write the basic information from which their representatives can draw. Arts galleries, institutions, and collectors will request them; websites (personal and institutional) typically will post them; applications and proposals will require them.

In other words: don't skip this chapter! It's a guide through a personal inventory, through the process of writing content. Writing inventories brings everything into place, making content as reachable as an artist's awl, brush, knife, pencil, or torch. The Artist Resume is the place to begin, the place to take inventory, because only the artist knows his background. The initial inventory process will take some time, but think of it as a template: once it's set up, it will be fairly easy to keep current.

Listing Accomplishments

It's probably a good idea to write the List of Accomplishments Worksheet (see p. 127) sooner rather than later, when there's time to work through the process. Have lists of accomplishments or something similar already on hand? Take this opportunity to update them. This inventory process is just another practical hurdle to clear!

This all sounds great, but where to start? The answer is deceptively simple: write lists. Check them twice.

- WHEN (most recent first)

- WHAT (degree, exhibition, award, grant, residency, other activity)

- WHO (Who gave or sponsored the degree, exhibition, award, grant, residency, or other activity?)

- WHERE (Where did it take place?)

- and more WHO (additional information such as jurors, sponsors, collaborators)

As always, this worksheet (p. 127) suggests ways to organize information. Please modify as needed. Whatever the format, spell-check and proofread each and every word. Double-check spellings of proper names and places. Keeping letter-perfect records will save a lot of time from editing (and reediting) future documents. Share the proofreading with a friend!

FINISHING

Think of proofreading as a final, finishing step; as something that every artifact deserves. Finished bronzes are waxed; finished charcoals are sprayed with a fixative; a two-dimensional work is prepared for installation on a wall. . . . These are final, time-consuming, but necessary steps to safeguard all of the work. Proofreading written drafts is exactly the same process.

The worksheet asks for basic information; namely, Education, Exhibition History, Awards, Grants, Residencies, and Press Coverage. For those involved in community projects, it would be important to add a Community Projects category. Best studio practices include writing things down when they happen, while all of the details are fresh.

The Artist Resume records the artist's accomplishments and exhibition history. It lists an artist's relevant accomplishments, exhibition history, and education. Items in a general resume that include work history—say, job titles and places of employment/commissions for a graphic designer who also exhibits art on occasion—do not belong in the Artist Resume.

Sometimes, artists have multiple resumes to meet professional demands outside the arts. A photographer with a day job as a fine art curator for a university gallery, for instance, might include an encyclopedic CV on her academic website.[2] The same photographer might have an Artist Resume just for her artist website. Similarly, the graphic designer who periodically exhibits ceramics might have two separate resumes for two separate websites, one promoting commercial work and another featuring ceramics. Typically, a short and sweet resume will do the trick.

⟳ 3 / p. 151

Maintaining a master resume, a document that is comprehensive, is highly recommended. Such a document can then be revised to meet specific deadlines or media (online or print). For instance, a new Artist Resume might include many more details about high school and undergraduate accomplishments; an emerging-career Artist Resume might be more selective, highlighting accomplishments such as exhibitions by placing them at the top of the page and concluding with education at the bottom of the page.

Finally: stick to the facts. Misrepresentation to get one's foot in the door may result in permanently mangling said foot.

The Artist Resume

Some standards for the Artist Resume include a header or letterhead complete with name, address, city, state, zip, artist website, email address, and telephone number. Only the artist can decide whether to include a specific street address. Those working from home studios might not want to publicly announce their private addresses for all the world to see. Others might want to publicize their addresses to encourage studio visits.

Reverse chronology is another standard. It follows hierarchical standards of visual representation, emphasizing most recent activities first and listing activities from previous years in descending chronological order.

That master resume will be most useful if the content is aligned on the left margin but remains unformatted: no tabs, bullets, numbers, or indents. Standard formatting means easy copying, pasting, and reformatting for online graphics or print for particular purposes—application, exhibition, or proposal.

AWARDS/GRANTS

2017

Name of Award, Host Institution, City, State

Name of Grant, Sponsor, City, State

2014

Name of Award, Sponsor, Host Institution, City, State

Readability is key to the Artist Resume. Note that using all CAPS, the dash, and the hard return at the end of the line can help distinguish between sections and entries.[3] Visible section headers that clearly mark information are most welcome. Remember, the Artist Resume is not an exhaustive CV that includes every single accomplishment. It is a resume; a one-page record of achievement in the arts. Some standards both for electronic and print resumes include

Length: one page

Margins: 1 inch or 0.75 inch

Point sizes: 11- or 12-point sizes

Typeface: Times New Roman, Tahoma, or Arial

A standard HTML, electronic-ready resume and its parts might look something like the HTML resume on the next page. If education, awards, collections, and other accolades exceed one page, a single page of Select Solo or Group Exhibitions can work well. Much will depend on the content of the List of Accomplishments or the Master Resume. For print Artist Resumes, sans serif typefaces such as Arial for headers and serif typefaces such as Times New Roman for content can increase readabililty. Limiting the number of typefaces to two—one for headers and perhaps another for content—is a generally accepted standard. Balancing white space, something that artists are expert with, also improves readability. Bullets, indents, italics, and bold can be used in the finished documents, but be selective. Hanging indents for text that goes beyond one line can be useful, too.

For widely accepted standards, the College Art Association (CAA), the nonprofit organization for art historians, studio art faculty, and graduate students, is reliable and easy to access.[4] The CAA's members collaborate to present standards within the arts. It is a tremendous resource about everything from copyright and fair use to career opportunities. When in doubt, explore the Standards and Guidelines section on the CAA website (www.collegeart.org).

A standard print Artist Resume and its parts might look something like the one on page 52.

A resume formatted for electronic submission might look something like this:

ARTIST NAME
somewhere, USA / email / website

EDUCATION
2015 MFA, Program (or emphasis), Institution, City, State
2013 BA, Program (or emphasis), Institution, City, State
2009 High School of the Arts, City, State

EXHIBITION HISTORY
Solo
-2015 Exhibition, Hosting Institution (or organization), City, State
-2010 Exhibition, Hosting Institution (or organization), City, State

Group
-2014 Exhibition, Hosting Institution (or organization), City, State
-2013 Exhibition, Hosting Institution (or organization), City, State

Invitational
-2015 Exhibition, Hosting Institution (or organization), City, State

Juried
-2015 Exhibition, Hosting Institution (or organization), City, State

AWARDS
-2010 Best in Show, Exhibition, Hosting Institution (or organization), City, State

INTERNSHIPS / RESIDENCIES
-2015 Title of Position, Hosting Institution (or organization), City, State

RELATED WORK
-2009 Title of Position, Hosting Institution (or organization), City, State

Sample resume formatted for electronic transmission.

ARTIST NAME
somewhere, USA / email / website

Education

2015   MFA, Program (or Emphasis), Institution, City, State
2013   BA, Program (or Emphasis), Institution, City, State

Exhibition History

Solo
2015   Exhibition, Hosting Institution (or Organization), City, State
2010   Exhibition, Hosting Institution (or Organization), Sponsoring Organization, City, State

Group
2013   Exhibition, Hosting Institution (or Organization), City, State T (Curated by _____,
        Title at Institution Name, City, State)

Invitational
2016   Exhibition, Hosting Institution (or Organization), City, State

Juried
2015   Exhibition, Hosting Institution (or Organization), City, State

Awards

2010   Best In Show, Exhibition, Hosting Institution (or Organization), City, State

Internships / Residencies

2015   Title of Position, Hosting Institution (or Organization), City, State

Related Work

2009   Title of Position, Hosting Institution (or Organization), City ST

(Ctrl) ▾

Sample student resume for print.

It's now time to turn to an emerging artist's sample resume. A former student, Morgan Dummit, was kind enough to share an early draft of his resume for publication in this book. Morgan's draft is unique in its content as well as in its formatting.

Note that the letterhead includes the artist's full name, website, studio address, cell phone number, and email address. It makes sense that Morgan, a sculptor, would include the address of his studio, although it's been redacted here to preserve his privacy. Other artists may prefer to exclude personal or specific information. Again, only the individual artist can know how much visibility or access he wants.

Just as the eye can be drawn to particular elements in an artwork, so too can the eye be drawn to particular areas of the written page. Morgan divided the resume into five clearly labeled sections to promote readability. Note how the consistent columns for information—one for place and another for dates—also make great use of white space. As an artist just starting to work, Morgan foregrounds his achievements by placing them on the reader-friendly left margin. Some line spacing is off-kilter in this draft, but it isn't anything that couldn't be quickly fixed in another revision. Looking for additional models of resumes? Check out the Maryland Institute College of Art's Career Resources for excellent instructional sheets and videos about building and designing resumes.[5]

An early career Artist Resume such as Morgan's will be fairly straightforward. Writing an emerging or midcareer Artist Resume will mean being more selective about the content, about what to emphasize. Thankfully, the Master Resume will have lots of information to help make the selection process easier!

MORGAN DUMMITT
Morgandummitt.com

Education

University of Pennsylvania, *Bachelor of Fine Arts*	Philadelphia, PA	2010-2013
Pennsylvania Academy of the Fine Arts, *Sculpture Major*	Philadelphia, PA	2009-2013
Florence Academy of Art, *Exchange Student, Sculpture*	Florence, Italy	Fall 2012
Art Students League of New York	New York, NY	2004-2009

Exhibitions

Annual Student Exhibition, Pennsylvania Academy of the Fine Arts	Philadelphia, PA	2013
Winter Juried Show, Pennsylvania Academy of the Fine Arts	Philadelphia, PA	2013
Annual Student Exhibition, Pennsylvania Academy of the Fine Arts	Philadelphia, PA	2012
Group Show, Christopher Street Financial	New York, NY	2012
Gallery 128, Pennsylvania Academy of the Fine Arts	Philadelphia, PA	2011
"Drawn from P.A.F.A", Chestnut Hill Academy	Philadelphia, PA	2011
"Annual Student Exhibition," Pennsylvania Academy of the Fine Arts	Philadelphia, PA	2011
"Towards the Future", New York Open Center	New York, NY	2011
"Anatomy/Academy," Pennsylvania Academy of the Fine Arts	Philadelphia, PA	2010
Gallery 128, Pennsylvania Academy of the Fine Arts	Philadelphia, PA	2010

Awards

The Perez Epstein Prize for Figure Modeling, Pennsylvania Academy of the Fine Arts	2012, 2013
The Lee Prize for Figure Drawing	2013
The Cook Prize for Figure Drawing	2012
Alumni Juried Award	2011

Publications

Cred Magazine	2011, 2012
The New York Times Arts Section	July 6 2011

Related Experience

Foundry Assistant, Studio of Shane Stratton	Philadelphia, PA	2010-2011
Foundry class assistant instructor, PAFA Continuing Education Program	Philadelphia, PA	2013
Foundry Assistant, Stanek Studios	Paulsboro, NJ	2013

Sample student resume for print.

The Artist Biography

The Artist Biography follows closely on the heels of the Artist Resume. It also features a fairly straightforward format that communicates the facts. Generic phrases for consideration include the following:

(Artist name) lives and works in _____. She received a ___ degree from _____ (year). Some of her recent exhibitions include _____, _____, and _____. She received the _____ award/prize/grant in (year). Her works are in a number of collections, including _____ and _____. _____ and _____ have reviewed her work.

The educational line, in this instance, identifying the source of the artist's degree, could read *interned*, *studied*, or *worked as a studio assistant*. If the template looks formulaic, it's because it is just that: a formula that works over and over again.

The Artist Biography focuses on the most-basic information found in the Artist Resume; namely,

- Name

- Place of residence

- Education

- Area of expertise

- Exhibitions and awards

- Bibliography

- Related experience

The Artist Biography translates biographical information and data from the resume into prose, highlighting the information that most generally describes the artist.

Let's mine Morgan's resume to draft a brief Artist Biography:

Sculptor Morgan Dummit lives and works in Philadelphia, Pennsylvania. In 2013, he received his BFA from the University of Pennsylvania and graduated from the Pennsylvania Academy of Arts. He also studied at the Art Students League of New York from 2004 to 2009. Both in 2012 and 2013, Morgan received the Perez Epstein Prize for Figure Modeling (PAFA). His work has been written about both in *Cred Magazine* and the *New York Times* Arts Section.

Impressive, right? As an Artist Biography, writing in the third person is the standard: the biography is about, not by, the artist. Note that the artist is alive and well: he lives and works. That active verb tense indicates current and relevant information. Keeping it short and sweet, say around 100 to 250 words, is highly recommended.

Emerging, midcareer, and established Artist Biographies will, of course, have much more information from which to draw. Some considerations would include:

- Place of birth

- Select solo or group exhibitions

- Select collections

- Current place of residence

- Special projects

- Publications

- Commissions

SAMPLE ARTIST BIOGRAPHY

Rochelle Weiner is a midwestern artist whose mediums include traditional watercolor, drawing, collage and monoprinting, and encaustic and oil / cold wax. Her subjects include abstract, landscape, the figure, and portraits.

Rochelle is now showing her work in Milwaukee at Café Lulu and Juniper 61, and in Chicago at the Leigh Gallery, the Andersonville Galleria, I Love Chicago on North Michigan Avenue, and at O'Hare Airport. Rochelle won honorable mention in the 2014 Watercolor Showcase national competition with *Watercolor Artist Magazine*, and her work will be published in the April 2015 issue of the magazine. Rochelle is a member of the ARC Gallery in Chicago, and she is also a member of the Illinois Watercolor Society, where she won honorable mention at the 2014 Members show and the "Award of Excellence" at their 2012 Members show, and she was juried into the 2012 national exhibition. Rochelle's work has been featured on the sets of NBC's *Chicago Fire*, NBC's *Chicago PD*, ABC's *Mindgames*, USA Network's *Sirens*, and the series *Sense8* on Netflix.

Rochelle has a bachelor's degree in painting and drawing from the University of Wisconsin–Milwaukee. She works professionally as the owner of Andiamo Creative, a full-service branding and web development company in Milwaukee. Rochelle recently moved back to her hometown, Milwaukee, Wisconsin, after 20 years living in Chicago.

Midcareer painter Rochelle Weiner's Artist Biography (see text box) gives basic information about her location, media of choice, gallery representation, awards, membership, and education. It's written in the third person, observes reverse chronology, and provided (in the original) links to the sources mentioned.

In short, it does exactly what it's supposed to do: communicate the credibility of the artist by highlighting career achievements. As these biographies demonstrate, the more polished the documents, the more professional and successful the independent artist appears.

Writing Process into Practice

Congratulations! The basic Artist Resume and Artist Biography are done, ready for updates as careers grow.

Make time for updates on a housekeeping schedule, that schedule of busy but necessary studio practice such as paying bills, ordering supplies, or prepping the studio.

These documents materially support the artist and her work in displays and exhibitions. The well-crafted Artist Resume and Artist Biography should be staples of any artist's studio practice, ready to be taken off the shelf and updated or revised whenever the need arises.

Throughout the rest of this book, readers will be asked to return to the List of Accomplishments completed in this chapter. It is hoped that these accomplishments will ground the reader in his areas of expertise, providing confident places from which to write about his work.

Notes

1. As mentioned elsewhere in this volume, not every independent artist is an entrepreneur, but every artist is self-employed. Those seeking education in business and marketing will be happy to find programs of study, and even combined MBA and MFA programs. For more analysis and information, see Beckman, "'Adventuring' Arts Entrepreneurship Curricula in Higher Education" (2007); Chang et al., "What Is Arts Entrepreneurship?" (2015); and Self-Employment in the Arts (www.selfemploymentinthearts.com).

2. The CV chronicles an academic's career. In addition to educational degrees, the scholarly CV lists academic appointments, departmental and professional affiliations and committees, publications, service to the academic and local communities, academic presentations, and so forth. Beyond these academic achievements, the CV for art studio faculty also includes items usually reserved for the artist resume: awards, grants, exhibition history, curated exhibitions, residencies, collections, commissions, interviews or feature articles, and so forth.

3. See Bhandari and Melber's *Art/Work* (2009) and Congdon's *Art Inc.* (2014) for additional examples and strategies for formatting Artist Resumes.

4. Career Resources (www.mica.edu/Academic_Services_and_Libraries/Career_Development/Career_Resources.html)

5. See Ricci, "Making a Statement," (2007) for insights from the National Association of Independent Artists.

Telling the Story: The Artist Statement

Everyone likes a good story. Everyone.

And no one tells that story better than the artist herself because no one knows the story better than the artist herself. Even those who write *about* art rather than *make* art require tutorials within art-historical analysis and art practice. And here's the very best news: research isn't required!

Some compare the written Artist Statement to a one-minute verbal elevator spiel.[1] The verbal elevator pitch, the TED Talk, and the written Artist Statement share the same objective: to communicate clearly and persuasively. Both for verbal and written modes of communication, all these standards apply:

- Make an excellent introduction / first impression.

- Create a story that engages and informs.

- Provide contact information.

For an artist, this might mean rattling off media or techniques during a chance encounter at a coffee house or an art opening. The analogy of the two-minute TED Talk applies as well: engaging in a quick and concise dialogue that gets the idea across without any fluff or filters. The objective: to communicate the enthusiasm an artist has for her work.

Being prepared for such opportunities might seem excessive, but there are times when being prepared for a chance meeting can make all the difference. Wouldn't it be great, for instance, if a jeweler launching a new line just happens run into the editor of *Ornament* magazine? Such encounters do, by the way, happen! The art world, when it comes right down to it, is a pretty small world.

Again: how an artist works may seem natural to an artist, but the rest of us really just don't know what's going on. And our curiosity makes us hungry for information. It stands to reason that explanations about motivation, process, research, and the like might be in order.[2] People need introductions, especially when they don't understand the visual cues.

In other words, art isn't always going to speak for itself. This is precisely where the Artist Statement comes into play. It is the opportunity to tell a story about a particular work or series in a Project Statement just like Kelli Hoppmann's compelling "Of Eight Balls and Dictionaries." The best part? An artist's statement is as inventive and as unique as the artist's singular vision.

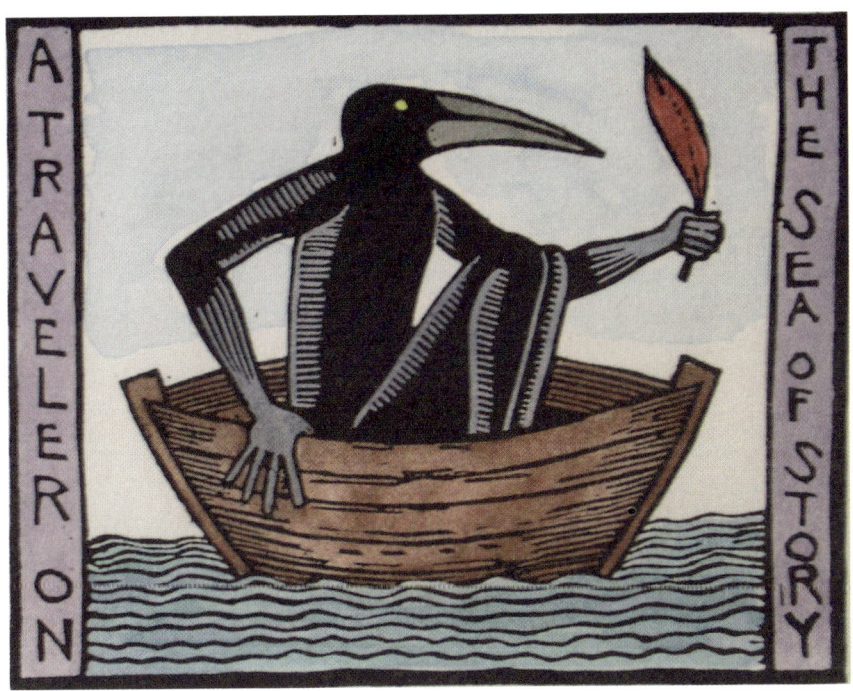

Marvin and Wendy Hill. *Traveler on the Sea of Story.*
Wood block print. © *Marvin Hill, 2017*

The Artist Statement

Artist Statements can be flowery, flagrant, high-falutin', fatiguing, or flat-out boring. They can be insightful, exciting, informative, or tantalizing. Typically, they don't exceed one typewritten page. Like the Artist Biography, the Artist Statement introduces the artist, the artist's intent or background, and the artist's appreciation for his own art to specific audiences. Artist Statements appear in applications, artist websites, exhibition catalogs, wall text descriptions in exhibitions, portfolios, proposals, press releases—the list goes on and on.

⟳ 4 / p. 152

The Artist Statement is an introduction to the hows and whys of an artist's work, not the last word. When done well, it leaves the reader wanting to know more, wanting to see more.

Exaggeration really just doesn't belong in an Artist Statement. Those who pursue such a path do so with peril. Nothing gets older or more stale in a shorter period of time than a bunch of baloney.

Artist Statements can give reasons for being an artist (what drives the artist, what thrills the artist), decisions the artist makes (about choices in media, subject matter, style), hopes for the future (creative, professional, personal), or any combination of the three. They are time sensitive, typically addressing current concerns. Thus, an Artist Statement written in 2018 won't tell a relevant story in 2020, though it might be a good place from which to pick up the narrative in 2022. In other words: updates required!

OF EIGHT BALLS AND DICTIONARIES

My father's father was a nasty drunk. He was every bad thing a man could be: violent, self pitying, irresponsible, arrogant, and mean. My grandmother divorced him in the middle of the Depression and moved into a one-bedroom apartment with nine children. They were better off.

Grandpa liked to read the dictionary and shoot pool. Pool is a beautiful game of the mind, the body, and the spirit that requires no special shoes. The dictionary is chock-full of meaning, by definition. I like to read the dictionary and shoot pool.

When reading the dictionary I find it best to have a big, fat dictionary that stays open to any page. It must be opened at random, of course. Sometimes you find themes running through it. The *re*'s are all full of second chances: rectify, reconstruct, reconsider, recover, re-create, redemption, reversal, redirect, relish . . . oops, we digress. The *im*'s can become a quagmire of negatives: immature, impatient, impossible, imprudent, impeach, impish; well, you see how it goes.

When I am composing paintings, the ideas are like words in search of definitions. My characters inhabit stages and parties. Look, over there is Anger, and Insolence just spilled a drink on him. I see Politics and Religion, the conjoined twins, and wonder "Who makes their clothes?" Can Hope get me through this insipid conversation with Denial? Malice just saw Charity from across the room and was heard saying, "Who invited her?" A wolf licks the breast of Desire in a dark corner; well, she is lovely. . . . They become costumes, gestures, animals, masks. They are studies of our follies, our plights, and our dreams.

The act of painting is like the pool game. A visual problem is presented; the mind measures angles, observes patterns, and forms strategies.

What touch must be employed? Soft? Hard? To the right? A little backspin? Where is it going to leave me? Then the fingers bridge and the arm releases one million paint-filled brushstrokes, until it is as natural as brushing your teeth. Finally you reach into your pocket to put more quarters on the table.

As it is with many good drunks, a doctor finally said to my grandfather, "Quit drinkin' or you'll die." So he went to Florida and walked the beach for two weeks. He walked, shook, slept, and walked. After that he never had another drink. He had the dog track and the Florida sunshine. What do you suppose that means. Maybe we can find the answer in the dictionary.

Kelli Hoppmann
(Artist Statement for exhibition Kelli Hoppmann: Dirt and the Clear Blue Sky; Courtesy of Abel Contemporary Gallery, 2017)

Personal Process + Practice Inventory

Before sitting down to write the story, take some time to think about creative process and practice. Just as brainstorming chapter 3's Lists of Accomplishments can produce content for the Artist Resume and Artist Biography, working on the Telling the Story: An Inventory Worksheet (see p. 132) can help artists visualize understandings about themselves, their craft, their practice, and their hopes and dreams. These worksheets help disrupt standard expectations by encouraging personal insights.

For the Inventory, try to write three to five thoughtful sentences in response to each prompt. Consider the "whys" or "hows"; describe what effect these elements have on the work. The more writing that occurs at this stage, the more selective the artist can be in crafting her story.

After completing the Inventory Worksheet, let a few days pass. Then give it another look. Remember the "Let it dry" stage in Charlotte Poehlmann's description of her creative process in chapter 2 (p. 21)? Taking a break from writing, letting it settle, can lend new perspective as well. Only the individual artist can make these connections clear in the Artist Statement.

Sample Artist Statement

Philadelphia Academy of Fine Art student Greg Biché wrote the following in my Business of Art seminar in Summer 2012 at University of Pennsylvania:

I draw and paint from observation. I do not set out to create an image; rather, I begin when moved by something I see. I draw when confronted with something that leaves me no choice but to draw. Compositions are not planned or created, but found; they are arrived upon somewhere in the process. Whether the wreckage of battle, the sloughed remains of growth, or the trail left behind exploration, my paintings are an artifact of the process of looking and describing what started the work in the first place. They are the result of efforts to keep myself surprised.

This is a pretty great first draft. We learn that Greg is a painter who likes to work from observing interesting, moving things in his environment.

Like many first drafts, there's a whole lot of "me" and the subject/verb sentence structure going on in these sentences. The use of the active verb tense (draw, do, begin, see), though, is to be highly commended. Note the shift in the latter half of the paragraph to the passive voice, to the verb "to be": "they are ...," "paintings are ...," "they are ...." This Artist Statement *tells* a lot about the artist and is dominated by the first-person pronoun in the opening sentences: "I draw ...," "I do ...," "I begin ...," "I see ...." The use of the first-person pronoun might seem repetitive, but it can be difficult to move beyond using it in an Artist Statement.

After some revisions, Greg's Artist Statement *shows* the development of his critical self-awareness. In the first paragraph of his 475-word final draft, for instance, his perception of his world remains central. He writes:

I draw and paint from observation, but not always directly. That is, both nature and artifice, both life and art: anything could compel me to draw. Ranging from five-centimeter drawings in ballpoint pen to oil paintings over five feet wide, my work takes its eventual form through a volatile process of observation and radical revision. The images are the artifacts of my attempts to communicate, my attempts to describe what I see. They comprise the act of looking made permanent.

Here, readers learn more about Greg's media and scale. Of course, the sophisticated variations of sentence structure are also welcome.

In the next paragraphs, Greg develops the theme of his evolving creative process even more. He writes, for instance, "I eschew fixed style, striving to keep any materials and techniques provisional; what worked last time, whatever tools or strategies I used on the last painting, are immediately suspect." Yet he's quick to let the reader know that "patterns that re-appear in what stimulates me, as well as systems that recur in my process. I'm drawn to clusters, scatters, scenes of disarray, moments of explosion or of slow decay." Greg's revised Artist Statement demonstrates that beyond anything else, he enjoys the work and finds the process of making stimulating. And that makes for a very engaging Artist Statement.

SIMPLIFY

Like the Artist Biography, concise and direct Artist Statements tend to pack a punch. Interested in increasing active voice? Find nominalizations— "introductions," "considerations," "evaluations"—and replace them with active verbs—"introduce," "consider," "evaluate." As these changes occur, many an "of," "for," "with," and additional words will fall by the wayside.

Another way to simplify prose is to find gerunds—"introducing," "considering," "evaluating"—and replace them with active verbs. When possible, that is. Sometimes alternatives to the verb "to be" (is, are, were) can be hard to find. Doing so, though, can improve tone and can shift to active voice. Such refining is like the Style Frames sequence noted in the Visual Poetics assignment in chapter 1.

Really hate the idea of the Artist Statement? Maybe think of it as a holdover from earlier times? Go ahead and write about *that*! The Artist Statement is all about sharing the artist's perspective. Please: have fun with it!

The core objective remains the same: to tell a good story. To repeat: Everyone likes a good story. Everyone.

Below is a really good story by midcareer painter Rochelle Weiner (Milwaukee, Wisconsin). Like many working artists, Rochelle has a day job.[3] Actually, "day job" is an inaccurate description: Rochelle owns a thriving graphic design design business. In addition to her Artist Biography and materials from her promotional packet (materials that will be featured in chapter 6), Rochelle granted permission to share her Artist Statement.

ARTIST'S STATEMENT

Background

After receiving my bachelor of arts in painting and drawing from UW-Milwaukee in 1992, I switched gears and started building a career for myself in graphic design. I worked in Milwaukee, London, and Chicago before starting my own graphic design company, Andiamo Creative, in 1998. During this time, I spent very little time painting—only working on occasional projects for gifts, or for the walls of my own home.

In 2010, I found my interest in painting reinvigorated by a weeklong watercolor workshop I'd taken on a lark. The week flew by. Afterward, I took stock and realized that the only times I've been so engrossed in something that I've actually lost time has been while I am creating art. I think these lost moments are doorways into your true soul, your passion as a human being, and the point of your existence on this earth. Through that door is boundless energy and creative juice. I have come to the realization that if you find this kind of thing in your life, you must go through that door.

Since then I have been painting regularly, showing my work, and pursuing a formal career in fine art.

Developing as an artist

In my journey developing my skills, I find that the main focus of my work has been about storytelling. The graphic designer in me is interested in illustration, and I started out in that direction. Also, I have a particular interest in the vintage snapshots that you find for sale in antique stores, and the lost stories of these people's lives. I can stand for ages sifting through bins full of discarded photos, wondering how these family memories ended up, now for sale. I started working these images into my work, and weaving narratives around them.

The mediums I have been working with—watercolor, encaustic, and cold wax, have a commonality in the transparency effects you can achieve. This transparency speaks to the storytelling that so interests me. The layering of color shows a history of the marks that compose the individual work, which adds to the fabric of the story. In addition, encaustic and cold-wax mediums have the unique property of allowing the artist to build up layers and texture, and to scrape back to earlier layers, revealing what had happened before. These techniques add both literal and narrative dimension to the piece, and interest to the stories I'm trying to tell.

While my first instinct has always been to paint recognizable imagery, over the last couple years I've also been developing an abstract series of work. Working in oil / cold wax, and the techniques I've been learning in the workshops, is particularly conducive to abstraction. I don't use paint brushes. Instead I use paint rollers, color-shaping tools, palette knives, and an array of mark-making tools to create these works. I have fallen in love with this medium and the freedom it allows me to break away from the constraints of imagery and create compositions that derive meaning purely from color, composition, line, and texture. The building-up of layers and then scraping back to reveal earlier layers speaks to my interest in storytelling. Each painting shows a history of what went before, even if in a very subtle way.

In conclusion

My main joy as an artist is the act of creation itself. I find inspiration all around me, every day. I used to say that my day job as a graphic designer sapped all the creativity out of me, leaving nothing for painting. I realize now what a cop-out that was. The real reason I hadn't painted in so long is because I didn't see a way to build a real career in fine art, and I felt I needed to spend my time building a stable income for myself. I learned that I needn't be so single minded, and that there are lots of ways to build a thriving career as a fine artist. And the most important thing I have learned is that the creative juice it takes for me to be a graphic designer is completely different from the juice I have for creating my own art. Happily, the jug overflows.

A Cautionary Tale

Students, maybe more than anyone else, know the perils that artspeak associated with contemporary art theory poses. Indeed, artspeak might be as heckled as academese:[2] the propensity of those within specialized fields to speak/write as though everyone else is within those specialized fields, to the exclusion of plain-speaking nonspecialists. As the previous sentences demonstrate, I hope, simple ideas can get complicated fairly quickly?

The satirical animation *How to Graduate from Art School* (November 18, 2013) by ProbCause depicts artspeak as incredibly pretentious and ultimately empty of meaning. According to the animation's caption, the work was "inspired by all the pretentious full[-]of[-]shit art school kids that I have the pleasure of going to graduate school with. For the last several months I have made a point to write down all the nonsense these students spit out during classes in critiques and format it into this monologue."

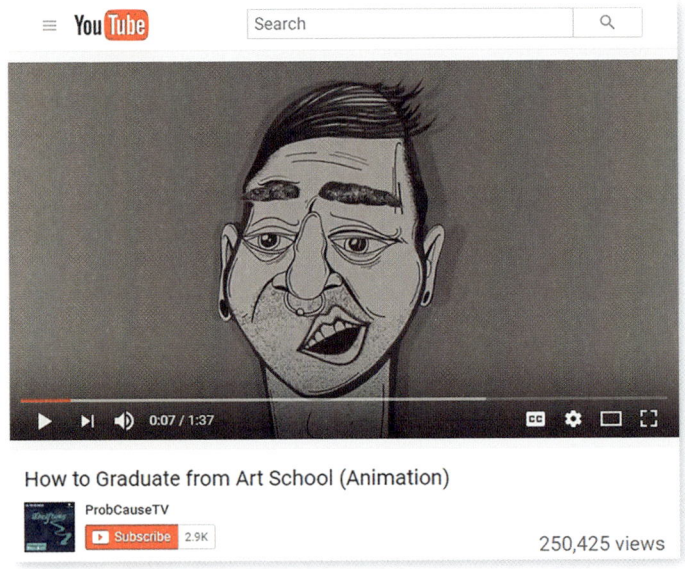

Screenshot of *How to Graduate from Art School* (animation). Animated, scripted, and performed by ProbCause, November 18, 2013, www.youtube.com/watch?v=T8RW7_dsW5Y.

It is worth transcribing the entire script for its finesse:

My practice is really about um, you know, um, like the ephemeral, um, and the temporal in, like, just this juxtaposition between gesture and text um and stillness and movement. . . . And, and, I really try to do it in a way that's, like, not overaestheticized because, like, I really want to evoke this pure sense of nostalgia for the viewer. But, but the viewer! I mean I don't even think about the viewer, cuz, I'm not like a sellout, heh. But, like, that brings like this whole idea of commodification in, like, America and like how society's so obsessed with consumption in capitalism. . . . But like I'm basically just using this, like, reductive process of visual style, but it's like not stylized because I'm like *not* a graphic designer like, like an *illustrator* or something. . . . But like my work is really about like the *non* objective. . . . Like at the end of the day, my work is really like an exploration of like Apollonian and and Dionysian . . . like these great dichotomies and like really unpacking these opposing forces in like you know exploring just like primal unity. You know?[3]

The satire is made even more pointed by the voice of the speaker in the animated video: imagine Beavis and Butt-Head, for instance. ProbCause's rant is at once hilarious and demoralizing, for the speaker does, in fact, know.

ProbCause masterfully repackages contemporary art theory into an engaging and satirical monologue. Note the keywords that appear in many an Artist Statement: juxtaposition, reductive, exploration, dichotomies. It's an exceptional gobbledygook of dialectical materialism, Marxism, psychoanalysis, postcolonialism, Nietzschean philosophy, and formalism. Please see *How to Graduate from Art School* on YouTube (www.youtube. com/watch?v=T8R@7_dsW5Y) to enjoy this animation in full.

BOLLOCKS

Additional examples of artspeak abound. Artybollocks.com, for instance, features an "Artybollocks Generator" for Artist Statements. Just click the button to get a personalized Artist Statement: "Do you hate to write your own artist statement? Generate your own artist statement for free, and if you don't like it, generate another one." Like the book, it identifies ways that statements might be useful: "funding applications, exhibitions, curriculum vitae, websites, . . ."[4] The site can help provide statements for Twitter, too.

Here's a closer look at an Artist Statement generated by Artybollocks. com on June 18, 2017:

> My work explores the relationship between postmodern discourse and unwanted gifts. With influences as diverse as Rousseau and Joni Mitchell, new synergies are created from both mundane and transcendant [sic] dialogues. Ever since I was a teenager I have been fascinated by the traditional understanding of the zeitgeist. What starts out as triumph soon becomes manipulated into a hegemony of lust, leaving only a sense of decadence and the prospect of a new beginning. As intermittent derivatives become transformed through diligent and repetitive practice, the viewer is left with an insight into the darkness of our future.

This sounds arty but pretty complicated, right? Sounds impressive, even. But what does it mean? Artybollocks.com takes a great deal of pleasure in the obscure. Here's a translation in plain speech:

> My work explores the relationship between high academic theory and making connections to the everyday, with influences ranging from French postimpressionist painting to folk music of the 1960s and '70s. These different elements collide, informing new perspectives. [Sentence 3 deleted; doesn't relate to preceding or following sentence.] I'm fascinated by how much best intentions can be derailed by daily realities, for better or worse. Mostly, I'm interested in learning what viewers think about my ongoing, rigorous practice.

ProbCause and Artybollocks fun aside, contemporary art theory has a place, particularly in academia and blue chip contemporary art galleries or museums. It might be expected at the innovative Mass MoCA (North Adams, Massachusetts), but visitors would find it difficult to navigate high theory at the more traditional cultural institution Wadsworth Atheneum (Hartford, Connecticut), a drive of just an hour or two down the road. Discussions among peers or during graduate seminars are integral to every artist's development. The question is how useful, or informative, such discussions might be for larger, art-appreciating, general audiences.

⮐ 4.1 / p. 152

Writing Process into Practice

Whatever creative and critical outlets the working artist draws on and writes is just fine. Journals, sketchbooks, paper napkins, backs of envelopes . . . anything that works, works. Writing about skills, methods, and processes in large part requires a degree of self-awareness. We know that artists report the positive impact when they regularly bring writing process into their studio practice.[5]

In any case, actually writing down reflections during the creative process can be useful.

Remember that first art show or exhibition? Remember feeling gratified by the compliments but anxious about sounding too egotistical when answering questions? For the seasoned artist (one hopes), that kind of anxiety has become a thing of the past. Like most things, the more practiced we become in visual and written communication, the more comfortable we become with expressing ourselves. Seasoned artists learn to share their excitement about their work, excitement that transfers really well to writing Artist Statements. Remember Greg Biché's first draft of the Artist Statement (p. 64) sprinkled with "me's"? As he revised and played with the genre, he shifted his perspective onto the story and ultimately generated a meaningful, polished Artist Statement.

Ready to write an artist statement or project statement? Think who, what, when, where, why . . . but not necessarily in that order.

- WHY: Why create? Why this particular project or series?

- WHAT: What are the motivating factors?

- WHO: Who will be reading this statement? General surfers of the web or arts specialists?

- WHEN: What's the statement's shelf life? Is it a general statement for the artist's website? Or does it reference a particular body of work?

- HOW + WHERE: Is it in print or online?

Take some time to think through these questions to generate ideas. Let them dry. Then dive into the writing process: propose, brainstorm, research, outline, draft, organize, complete draft, give feedback, finalize draft!

Notes

1. Grant, *The Business of Being an Artist* (2010).
2. Pinker gives academics a run for their money in "Why Academics Stink at Writing" (2014).
3. Transcription provided in a personal correspondence by the artist behind ProbCause, Colin Grimm.
4. Artybollocks Generator (http://artybollocks.com/, accessed June 18, 2017).
5. Collinson, "Artistry and Analysis: Student Experiences of UK Practice-Based Doctorates in Art and Design" (2005).

Applying Yourself

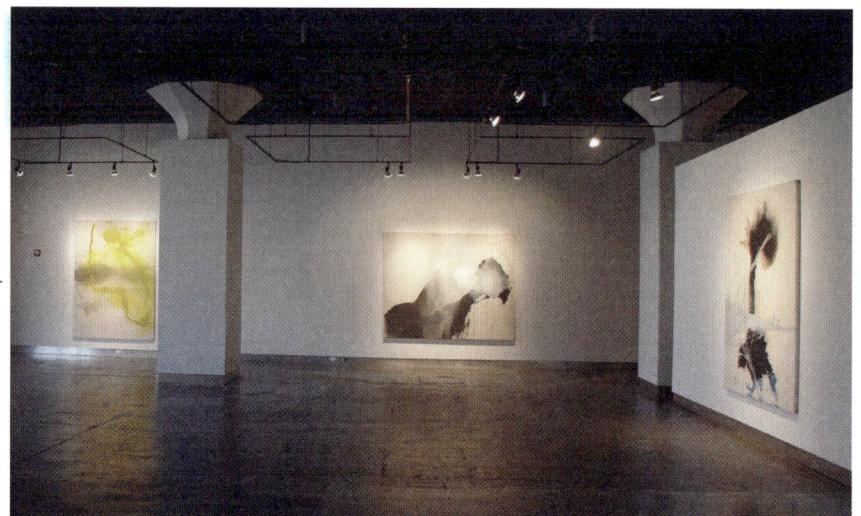

Installation view of Greg Klassen exhibition *Perishable Atlas* at INOVA
(Institute of Visual Arts), University of Wisconsin–Milwaukee, 2011.

That commission, exhibition, fellowship, grant, or residency won't come knocking on the studio door all by itself. Artists need to apply, and to apply mindfully. All the research completed thus far should give the artist insights into writing the applications: the homework is done (chapter 2), content for the Artist Resume and Artist Biography are on file (chapter 3), and at least ideas about material for the Artist Statement (chapter 4) are in the works.

Ultimately, applications are great opportunities to get to know places and people that might otherwise feel intimidating. Once an artist becomes affiliated with any highly respected organization, she shares in its prestige, gaining credibility with peers and a savvy art community.

Becoming a member of arts organizations, talking to peers, sharing resources, subscribing to listservs and arts journals—all these strategies can lead to opportunities, some of which will be explored in this chapter.

In any case, doing the research to find the right fit is an important first step.

Juried Exhibitions

Submitting work to juried exhibitions is just another way to get work circulating in art communities. Like everything else, do the research first. Research to learn about the host institution, the event, and the jurors' backgrounds and expectations.

Paying particular attention to the caliber of the juror (or jurists) has its own rewards. Notable figures frequently serve as jurors: curators, directors, collaborators, writers, collectors. Going through the jury process can have unforeseen positive results beyond the juried activity itself. The submitted work might not find a place in an exhibition, for instance, but it might appeal to a juror who's looking for artists for another project.

Deadlines and descriptions for juried exhibitions as well as other funding opportunities are posted in many places. Here are a few:

Organization	Website
CaFÉ	www.callforentry.org
Professional Artist Magazine (formerly *Arts Calendar*)	www.professionalartsmag.org
Artist Deadlines	www.artistdeadlines.com
American Artist	www.americanartist.us
Art Fair Calendar	www.artfaircalendar.org.

The key? Matching the work to the Call for Artists and following instructions.

⟳ **5 / p. 153**

If the Call for Artists specifies 2-D work only, for Pete's sake don't submit 3-D work. Send no less and no more than what is requested. If three images are requested, send three images; if email submissions are discouraged, don't submit the application via email. To fail to follow directions is to jeopardize one's reputation.

It's important to deliver on the promise. If a jury approves an impressionistic painting but the artist sends an abstract oil, the organizer will be annoyed and will likely withdraw the abstract oil from the exhibition.

Some artists balk at such expectations. They ask, Why wouldn't the newer abstract oil be more interesting than the older impressionistic painting? The answer: The submitted work is the approved work. Only. Period. For the organizers, protecting the integrity of their show is imperative. Submitting bait (such as the impressionistic painting) to gain entry and then switching to an alternative media or style (such as the abstract oil) wouldn't serve anyone well.

Once accepted, the thrill of preparing the work for exhibition and of adding the exhibition to the Artist Resume will be justly earned. If denied? Don't get too discouraged! Convinced it's the best place to exhibit work? Put the event application date on next year's calendar; review criteria, organization, and jurors again; redouble efforts; and reapply.

Grad School, Grants,
+ Other Great Expectations

Before the application process can begin, the individual artist needs to take a lot into consideration, including areas of expertise, location, and career stage; financial and time commitments; and opportunities for expanding knowledge or for collaboration, and so forth. Ready to proceed? Thinking this through with the Priorities Worksheet will help sort out some key issues (see p. 138).

Once the Priorities Worksheet is done, start exploring websites for information. Searching for specific opportunities (e.g., watercolor juried exhibitions in Ohio) can help keep the search process focused, although going on tangential internet searches (e.g., international watercolor juried exhibitions) can yield unexpected and happy results.[1]

Here are a few websites that post exhibition, funding, legal, and residency opportunities:

Organization	Website
ARTinsight	www.artinsight.org
CaFÉ	www.callforentry.org
Creative Capital	www.creative-capital.org
Fractured Atlas (New York City)	www.fracturedatlas.org
New York Foundation for the Arts	www.nfya.org
ResArtis	www.resartis.org

Of these, ARTinsight is perhaps the most useful one-stop shop. It features an extraordinarily user-friendly alphabetical listing of grant opportunities and shares business advice about law, taxes, business practices, and copyright.

Looking for grants, teaching, fellowships, and residencies? These are all good places to start:[2]

Organization	Website
American Alliance of Museums	www.aam-us.org
Americans for the Arts	www.americansforthearts.org
American Council of Learned Societies	www.acls.org
College Art Association	www.collegeart.org
Duke Research Funding	www.researchfunding.duke.edu
Fulbright Scholars	www.cies.org
HigherEdJobs	www.higheredjobs.com
H-Net (Humanities Net)	https://networks.h-net.org
National Endowment for the Arts	www.arts.gov/grants
National Endowment for the Humanities	www.neh.gov/grants/
National Gallery of Art	www.nga.gov/content/ngaweb.html
Philanthropy News Digest	www.philanthropynewsdigest.org

In the US, individual state departments of the arts or cultural affairs, the National Parks Artist Residencies (www.nps.gov/subjects/arts/air.htm), and US Government Grants (www.grants.gov) are great gateways to exhibition and funding opportunities. Likewise, the arts councils for provinces in Canada as well as the Canada Council for the Arts (www .canadacouncil.ca) are excellent resources.

Find that perfect match? The Research Worksheet (See p. 140) shows how to analyze a host or sponsor mission. Missions, programs, procedures, and contacts provide invaluable information and are easy to access on websites.

The Analysis Worksheet (See p. 142) helps analyze the content on the website through a careful reading of keywords, vocabulary choices, level of formality, and so forth. It helps pay attention, for instance, to the word choices, sentence structure, and overall tone of the website content; keywords can be borrowed for a cover letter or project description. These worksheets will help bring an organization into clear focus.

Kansas.gov: A Case Study

On October 24, 2014, the Kansas.gov website yielded the following links for "art" in its search field:[3]

Kansas Board of Healing Arts

Kansas Arts Commission

Kansas Board of Healing Arts License Renewal

General opportunities in the arts as opposed to the specialized healing arts seemed most interesting, so the "Kansas Arts Commission" link was selected:

Visual Arts—Kansas State Department of Education

Cool Things—Modern Ledger Art, Kansapedia

Art Galleries-Museums

Kansas Department of Commerce—Official Website

Kansas Creative Arts Industries Commission (CAIC)

After following the multiple links (some to dead ends), a link to the pot of gold at the end of the rainbow appeared: the CAIC.

According to the website, "The Kansas Creative Arts Industries Commission (CAIC) is focused on the creative industries sector of the Kansas economy. The Commission is dedicated to measuring, promoting, supporting, and expanding the creative industries to grow the state's economy and create creative industry-related jobs." The CAIC page is a treasure trove of information about funding opportunities, including grants and film resources for industry, arts organizations, and education.

The link to the Mid-America Arts Alliance (MAAA) revealed a regional consortium supporting the arts created by Arkansas, Kansas, Missouri, Nebraska, Oklahoma, and Texas. Mural programs, exhibition support, performing-arts touring, professional and community development, and a collaboration with the National Endowment of the Arts all are supported by the MAAA. Noodling around some more showed that while the awards topped out at $15,000, additional awards were available throughout the year.

Finally, write the findings down. Interested in pursuing public art? It might be worthwhile to review the Case Study for a public art application. It provides a step-by-step analysis of a call for proposals (CFP) (see p. 113).

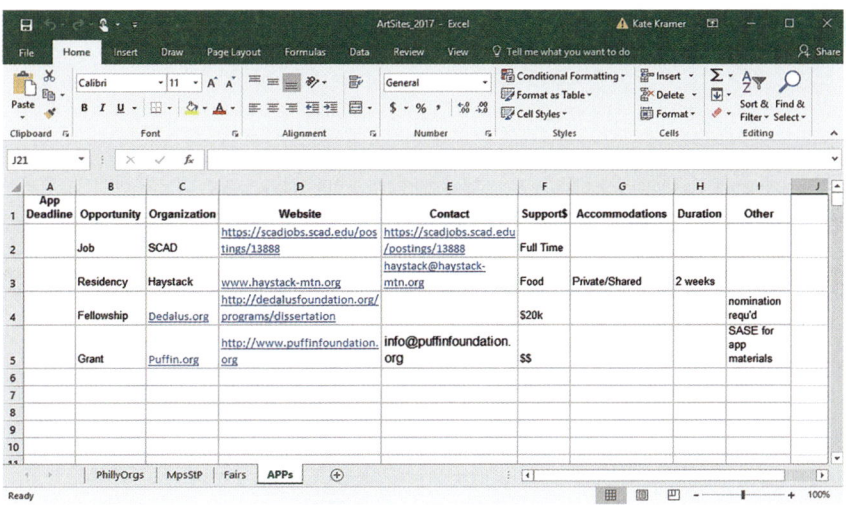

Remember the ArtSites_2017 Excel workbook that started in chapter 2? This worksheet (Apps) organizes search results by employment, residency, fellowship, and funding. Later, these categories can be grouped together by a quick alphabetical sort. Only the individual artist can know what categories to use. Here's something that can't be emphasized enough: follow the directions for any and all applications to the letter. Applications and proposals are never, repeat NEVER, one size fits all. The Case Study for the public art application may serve as a model of careful reading in this regard (see p. 113).

- If a particular format for the proposal or project statement is specified—say three pages, single spaced, 12 point or larger as a .doc or .pdf—submit a three-page, single-spaced, 12-point at least .doc or .pdf. Period.

- If digital images in .jpeg format with 350 dpi are requested, submit images in the specified format.

- If using headers, bullets, or both is recommended to organize key elements, do it.

- If a hard deadline is published, observe it. Deadlines hold fast for most grants and programs. The good news: if a deadline is missed in one cycle, the application can be pursued in the following cycle. Just remember to add it to the calendar.

- If a Cover Letter, Artist Resume, Artist Biography, Artist Statement, images, and accompanying image list describing work samples are requested, provide them.

In short, do exactly as asked. No less, no more. For the reviewers, the whole review process can be overwhelming. Make it easy on them! Stand out from the crowd for the art as well as for the professionalism.

Some Standards

Standard documents—such as budgets, proposals, and project descriptions—will be requested, but keep a close eye on specific objectives and submission methods. The criteria are specific on purpose. Applications that don't match the criteria end up in the trash can, wasting the applicant's as well as the reviewer's time. Like the rubric category in the VisualPoetic assignment in chapter 1, application and proposal criteria describe key components and objectives. Proposals that meet preferred criteria stand better chances of success.

Getting ready to submit the proposal? Remember to contact references to remind them of the project, to share links to the announcement with them, and to ask if they're familiar with or have had previous experience with the host organization and its representatives. It never hurts to ask!

Depending on the application, the Cover Letter and Project Statement might be one and the same. Ultimately, both documents demonstrate the following:

- What the applicant proposes to do

- How the applicant proposes to do it

- Why the project is important

- Who will benefit in the long term—host, discipline, applicant?

The "what" section tends to be briefer than the remaining sections. The "how" might involve multiple components. The more distinct the differences between the "why" and the "who," the better.

Cover Letter

After doing the research, identifying how to make connections between an artist's project and an organization's goals should be clearer. Being able to explain these connections is central to that first impression: the Cover Letter.

COVER LETTER STANDARDS

[In absence of letterhead, provide the following at the top left of the letter]

Artist First Name, Last Name
Address
City, ST Zip Code

Organization Name
Contact Name or Title
Address
City, ST Zip Code

Date

Re: Event or opportunity

Dear ___:

[if justified left margin, one return between paragraphs; if indenting first lines of paragraphs, returns between paragraphs unnecessary]

Introductory Paragraph:
Simply state interest in whatever is being offered. Identifying familiarity with or similarities between the event, key figures, or organization might also be interesting tacks to take.

Second Paragraph:
Typically, a brief (350 word) abstract, or summary, of a Project Statement might be useful here.

Third Paragraph:
Thank the reviewer(s) for their time and consideration.

Closing:
"Sincerely" tends to be the most professional. "Best" is acceptable if the writer has a personal relationship with the receiver.

If possible, share the letter with a friend to check on readability and to proofread final copy! Clean grammar and clear prose will go a long way toward establishing respect. The Cover Letter ought to be written just before submitting the actual proposal; only then will the artist be able to reflect on all the work that has gone into the proposal itself.

Project Statement

Like the Cover Letter, the Project Statement is audience specific. And, as with the Cover Letter, the applicant knows that audience well if the research has been thorough. Tell the story that will help reviewers understand the proposal's importance and its relevance to the host's mission or objectives. Use that knowledge! Address that audience! Strive to demonstrate interest in and knowledge about the host institution as sincerely as possible.

Thank You for Your Interest, But . . .

And about those rejections: first, review the criteria (yes, again!) and compare them to the application. Make a self-critical assessment. Did the application adequately address the criteria? Did it follow instructions to the letter?

If the opportunity still seems relevant, redouble efforts. Go for it again. Then put it on the calendar and reapply during the next review cycle.

Sometimes, the third time really is the charm. Some granting institutions have reputations for keeping an eye on repeat applicants and how their applications evolve with each submission. If each submission significantly and sincerely improves on the last and strives to meet the criteria, it would seem that such efforts would be time well spent.

Writing Process into Practice

"Applying Yourself" is the trifecta of *Artists Write to Work*. Readers put it all into practice by bringing it all together. They've done the homework, taken the inventory, written their stories, and prepared to put themselves out there on the line.

Just like maintaining a calendar for web updates, keeping a routine schedule of opportunities might be the best way to bring the application process into practice. Set a date each month to see new calls for applications.

UNCLE SAM

There's one more place that can provide important information about any particular nonprofit organization in the United States: the International Revenue Service. Yes! The IRS.

The government requires nonprofits to submit a 990 form that identifies major contributors and revenues and that records salaries over $50,000, assets, expenditures, awards, and names of award recipients. The 990 thus makes it possible to know who has received awards in the past three years and what amounts have been granted. Guidestar.org and National Center for Charitable Statistics (www.nccs.urban.org) give basic—and free!—access to 990s. Researching 990s is nothing but time well spent.

Test Run:

A random look at the Aaron Siskind Foundation's Individual Photographer's Fellowship (IPF) is pretty instructive. The IPF award grants up to $10,000 on an annual basis to recipients. The gracious application time frame — from mid-May to mid-July—gives interested applicants plenty of time to do some research, right? The website (www.aaronsiskind.org/grant.html) shares important information about past recipients and judges as well as an invaluable FAQs section for IPF applicants. All good information.

If information about individual recipients or judges wasn't available on the website, the 990 would have been a great place to find out more information about the people involved. In this case, the 990 lets us know that the IPF awards were made to four or five recipients in the amount of $8,000 each between 2012 and 2014.

Miss a deadline? Put a reminder on the next month's/quarter's/year's calendar.

Applying oneself is time consuming. It takes a great deal of commitment to work all the way through application processes. Only the individual artist knows how long it will take to write an application, and whether the time dedicated to pursuing a proposal is worth it in the long run.

Here is a review of the recommended process:

❶ Complete the Priorities Worksheet

❷ Research online

❸ Complete the Research Worksheet

❹ Write it all down

❺ Write drafts

❻ Follow directions

❼ and ... Submit!

Knowledge is indeed power: the more the applicant can speak to a particular audience with its particular objectives and understandings in mind, the better. The Cover Letter is the handshake, the elevator impression. And it's all in writing.

Notes

1. Peterson's (www.petersons.com/search/) is a good source for information about graduate school programs.

2. The Fulbright Scholar Program (www.cies.org) provides a lot of guidance for the proposal process, including sample Project Statements and webinars.

3. Creative Arts Industries Commission (www.kansascommerce.com/caic, accessed October 24, 2014)

Broadcasting the Word

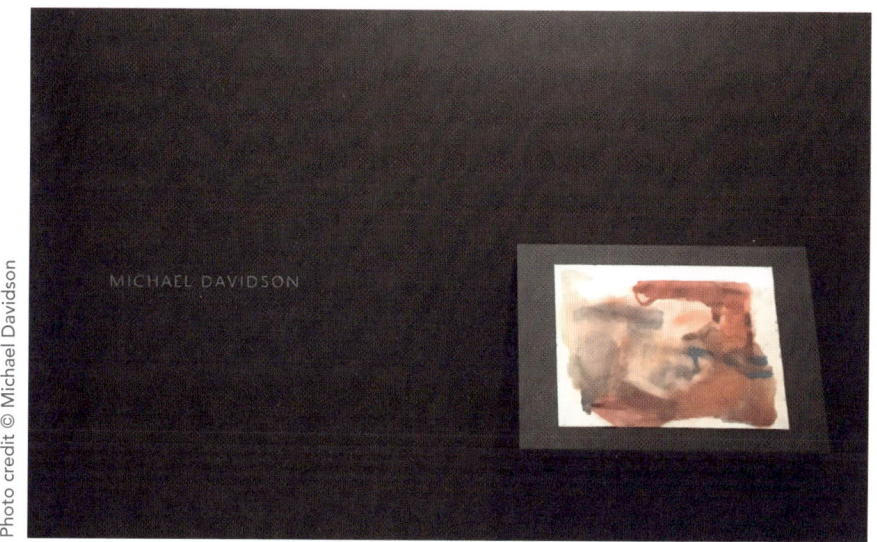

Installation view of title wall for *Michael Davidson* exhibition, the Re Institute, Millerton, New York, fall 2016.

Just like it's important to explore a range of opportunities, it's important to broadcast the word far and wide. And the independent artist has a range of indie activities—open studios, gallery tours, street fairs, organized and outsider art and craft fairs, art residencies at area K–12 schools—that she can promote. In today's digital age, well-written press releases to broadcast the word are more important than ever.

The good news: the Press Release, like the Artist Resume and Artist Biography, has fairly fixed standards. These standards make the Press Release easy to write as well as easy to distribute. Standards include a descriptive banner, pertinent information, larger narrative description of event, contact information, and excellent visuals. Think who, what, when, and where. The Press Release has the added advantage of having staying power: it provides content for invitations, announcements, and wall text for exhibitions and formally archives the event itself.

Well-crafted Press Releases make it easy for publications to lift content, with banners and descriptions that can be copied and pasted. This is more important than ever because many news organizations no longer have anyone on staff to write such notices. Reproducible, high-resolution images increase the chance of being printed or circulated electronically: black and white for newsprint, color for internet and glossy magazines. A gallery might write a press release itself, but it will need the artist to provide content—like the Artist Statement, Resume, and Biography—as well as reproducible, high-quality images, and maybe even a quote to include in the release.

Standards

Unlike any other document for the business of art, the Press Release is double spaced and can be longer than one page. Like the Artist Resume, the material is placed in descending order of importance, from top to bottom, privileging visual hierarchies of scale. It will look something like page 89.

The Press Release, addressed to the calendar or arts editor, should appeal for its newsiness. In many cases, publications will virtually lift the content of the Banner, the first paragraph, and details from the closing paragraph. Many print media and online publications now prefer online press release submissions, providing entry boxes with character limits. Such limits make decisions about prose style short work for the press release writer!

The quality of images is also important. The higher the quality of the images, and the more the size of the images fit with the receiver's specifications, the better the chance of publication. (See Press Release Worksheet, p. 144.)

On a practical level, include the copyright credit for the image in the Press Release. If information about the image—the artist, title, media, size, and date of the work of art—is included, chances are that it will appear in print. If it's not possible to include an image when submitting the Press Release, the tagline "Images available upon request" can always be added to the bottom of the Press Release.[1]

By the way: when a Press Release is reprinted word for word, take it as a compliment. In the land of media, such copying is not plagiarism—where someone else gets credit for someone else's writing—but a standard necessity. For a sample press release in the context of a complete promotional packet, please see the Case Study: Fine Art Gallery Exhibition (see p. 108).

FOR IMMEDIATE RELEASE

Date:

Contact: Name, title, institution; email; telephone number

BANNER: One sentence summary of event

Blurb paragraph: Two- to three-sentence explanation of Banner highlights

Paragraph 1: Who, what, when, where

Who will host the event? Where and when will it take place (date and time)? What is significant about the event? Who are some of the noted participants (or who is the coordinator/organizer/host of the event)?

Paragraph 2: What and why (justify why it's newsworthy)

Paragraph 3: Possible continuation of paragraph 2

Paragraphs 3/4: Details about access, directions, and host:

(Title of event) will run from (dates). Admissions (determined by host). The host is open (days and times), excluding (holidays, Mondays, etc.). (Host institution one-line blurb here.)

(Coordinator/organizer one-line blurb here.) Please contact (repeat information in header) for more information and directions.

Image credit ____.jpeg / Artist name. Title of work. Media. Date / Photo credit ___.jpeg

Copyright artist or name of photographer, date.

###: End of release

Rochelle Weiner, midcareer artist and author of the Artist Statement featured in chapter 4, shared this Press Release:

❶ F O R   I M M E D I A T E   R E L E A S E

❷ AUGUST 10 2015
Rochelle Weiner Fine Art
Milwaukee WI

❸ CONTACT:
Rochelle Weiner
773 609 0008
rochelle@rochelleweiner.com

----

❹ East Side Milwaukee artist returns home after 20 years in Chicago

❺ Rochelle Weiner is an award winning contemporary artist, recently returned to Milwaukee, her hometown, after working and residing for 20 years in Chicago. She is now showing her abstract series, "Strata+Sphere", at Lulu's Cafe in Bay View and Juniper 61 in Wauwatosa.

Showing through October 2015
❻ Lulu's Café and Bar
2261-2265 S Howell Avenue
Milwaukee WI

Showing through January 2016
Juniper 61
6030 W North Avenue
Wauwatosa, WI

❼ *"It's surreal to be an East Sider again after being away for so long - so much has changed yet much has remained the same. Twenty years ago I moved to Chicago to expand my career opportunities. Now I've moved back into my family home, and I'm setting up an art studio in my old bedroom."*

❽ Rochelle's main interest in painting lies in storytelling. Her "Strata+Sphere" series of abstract works uses layered painting techniques to depict abstract memories of growing up on Milwaukee's East Side. The layered painting methods that she has developed - using opaque and transparent mediums to build up layers of color and texture, scraping and washing back to reveal earlier layers and then building up and covering up again, shows a history of what went before, even if in a very subtle way. This tells a story both of her painting process and of her subject matter. She works in varied mediums to achieve her goals, including watercolor on aquabord, oil/cold wax on board, watercolor and powdered charcoal on paper.

❾ Rochelle hopes that the paintings will stir memories for those who lived in Milwaukee through the 70s and 80s. Titles like "Downer Ave Bike Race", "Snake Hill", and "Meet me at Bradford Beach" may be of some help. *"This is a series about memories of growing up in Milwaukee in the 70s and 80s. There's a painting currently hanging at Juniper 61 called "Painting Kowalski's Wall". This title refers to a day when I was about 7 years old. My friend Laurie and I took a can of grey house paint and some brushes from my parent's basement, hid behind a bush on Bradford and Downer right by the bus stop, and started painting the brick wall of the building there. A neighbor spotted us and alerted my mother – which quickly ended our fun. I got in big trouble for that caper. The bushes we hid behind are no longer there, but you can still see the grey paint on that wall today."*

"The painting called "Sr Agnes Marie", currently hanging at Lulu's, is about my 1st *grade teacher. She was a tiny, angry nun who taught at Sts Peter and Paul in the days when nuns could still get away with corporal punishment in the classroom. I was*

never the recipient of her anger, but I saw some kids get their heads rapped against the blackboard when they misbehaved. You did not want to mess with Sr Agnes Marie."

Rochelle Weiner studied painting and drawing at the University of Wisconsin-Milwaukee and works professionally as owner of Andiamo Creative, [ANDIAMOCREATIVE.COM], a full service branding and web development company now relocated to Milwaukee. Rochelle shows her work in Chicago at The Leigh Gallery, the Andersonville Galleria, and I Love Chicago on North Michigan Avenue and at O'Hare Airport. Rochelle won honorable mention in the 2014 Watercolor Showcase national competition with Watercolor Artist Magazine and her work was published in the April 2015 issue. She is a member of the ARC Gallery in Chicago, and is also a member of the Illinois Watercolor Society, where she won honorable mention at the 2014 Members show. She was given the "Award of Excellence" at their 2012 Members show, and was juried into the 2012 national exhibition. Rochelle's work has been featured on the sets of NBC's Chicago Fire, NBC's Chicago PD, ABC's Mindgames, USA Network's Sirens, and Sense8 on Netflix. Rochelle's work can be viewed online at rochelleweiner.com and facebook.com/RochelleWeinerFineArt. Rochelle Weiner is currently seeking gallery representation in Milwaukee.

Image list © Rochelle Weiner

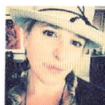
Portrait of Rochelle Weiner

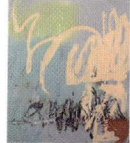
"Painting Kow

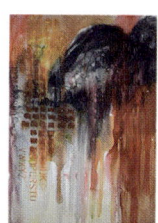
"Sr Agnes I

❶ Modified Letterhead

❷ Date

❸ Contact Information

❹ Banner

❺ Blurb: who, what, where, when

❻ Details: what, when, and where

❼ Quote from artist: why / begins a story

❽ Explanation: who, what, how, why

❾ Details: relates explanations to particular images

⑩ Artist Biography: who (the artist) and why (significant accomplishments)

Milwaukee's weekly paper the *Shepherd Express* clearly liked Rochelle's Press Release so much that it published a blurb in addition to putting it on its calendar listings just eight days after receiving it.

"Strata+Sphere". . . Ever since Odysseus spent 10 years getting waylaid on his way back to Ithaca after 10 years fighting in the Trojan War, the theme of homecoming has been ubiquitous in art and literature. Native Milwaukeean Rochelle Weiner is a revenant recently returned to the East Side after 20 years of twists and turns in Chicago.

"Strata+Sphere" presents a series of abstract works using layered painting techniques to capture memories of growing up on Milwaukee's East Side. The show straddles two locations with larger canvases at Lulu's in Bay View through October and small/medium-sized works at Wauwatosa's Juniper 61 through January 2016.[2]

While the writer Tyler Friedman took the time to write engaging copy about the exhibition, he also borrowed from Rochelle's prose. Note how the second paragraph condenses information from Rochelle's banner, and the second paragraph addresses a central theme in Rochelle's work: storytelling. The *Strata+Sphere* Press Release and the text in the *Shepherd Express* demonstrate how an effective release can gain press attention.

Timing

Timing, as the saying goes, is everything. Keeping track of different timelines for different media outlets is yet another thing to put on the calendar. Successful planning for releases can lead to successful multimedia coverage over a period of time.

Three to four months prior to event

Monthly popular, regional, and shelter publications typically plan their issues three to four months in advance. Thus, timely submissions to the calendar and arts editors stand a good chance of getting into print. It also gives the arts contact enough time to put the event on the calendar and maybe make it to the event itself.

To find out about upcoming editorial themes that might coincide with an event (food, gender, conservation), check out the "For Advertisers" section on a publication's home page. If the event works well with the editorial calendar, there might be opportunities for feature articles or interviews as opposed to just calendar listings. Sections with information for advertisers are really valuable: they frequently provide specific information about the demographics of a publication's audience.

Ten to fourteen days in advance of activity

Local weekly calendars tend to schedule ten to fourteen days in advance.

Seven to ten days in advance of activity

Daily newspapers and local TV and radio tend to have the shortest lead times.

Miss a deadline? Go ahead and send the press release with an invitation to the appropriate staff member. Titles and duties can usually be found on the "About," "Contact," or "Staff" sections on a website.

Please double-check these general time frames well before an individual marketing campaign begins. The more timely the distribution of promotional materials, the greater the possibility of getting press coverage. Keep an eye on timeliness when it comes to mailing postcards or sending emails as well. Nothing, repeat NOTHING, is more disappointing than receiving an announcement a day, week, or month after the fact.

A well-timed campaign can maximize press coverage before, during, and after an event. Of course, successful pop-ups get great press during and after the events too. Sharing announcements that include the details and contact information at any event can help keep the momentum going.

Press Release Byproducts: Recycling Content for Support Materials

Just as an artist will reuse raw materials—canvas, metal, wood, clay—in his studio, so too will he recycle content from the Press Release for promotional materials. Writing that Press Release well in advance of an event has the added advantage of checking off items on the "To Do" list well before event activities get hectic. When it's time to install an exhibition, it's a relief to have well-written material ready to go.

It's pretty easy (and effective) to copy from the Press Release and paste into other promotional materials such as postcard invitations, flyers, email announcement blasts, posters, and wall text. The Press Release thus deserves attention before and during event planning. The more all of these promotional elements relate to one another to broadcast the word, the better.

Paragraph 2 of the Press Release—the what and the why of the event—can be edited down for use in an invitation, for instance. Just as the Artist Statement provides the content for the elevator pitch on which artists can rely during face-to-face encounters, the second paragraph provides the content for a pitch about the event. If an event includes lots of artists, such as an Open Studio public event, such a pitch has the added advantage of keeping the message consistent for everyone involved. In other words: no surprises!

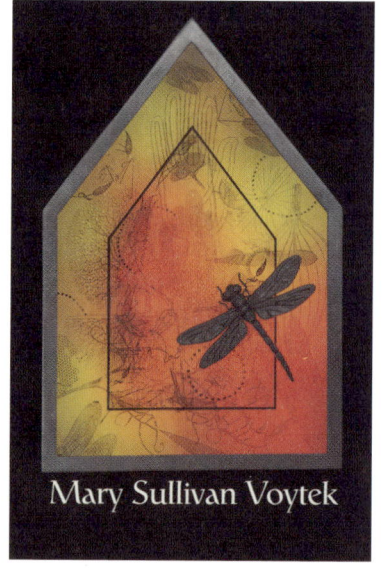

Mary Sullivan Voytek exhibition postcard invitation, Eclectic Electric Gallery, Atlanta, Georgia, 2003.

Mary Sullivan Voytek

Conceptually, accessibility and visibility unify all print and promotional materials. The Press Release first announces an event and then archives it on host organization and artist websites. The invitation privately invites participants and can be shared with relevant arts-and-media networks. Its content can be graphically organized to appeal to a wide audience if it includes high-quality images, narrative prose, or even a bulleted list of activities or artists, and so forth. Only the individual artist can anticipate which promotional materials will work best for his audience.

The Writing's on the Wall

Some artists consider wall text at art exhibitions as overkill. After all, isn't a picture worth a thousand words? Wall text, they maintain, distracts an admiring public from the main objective: to see the art! Indeed, it can be frustrating when the body of a well-meaning visitor blocks the view of a work of art because she's reading the adjacent wall text.

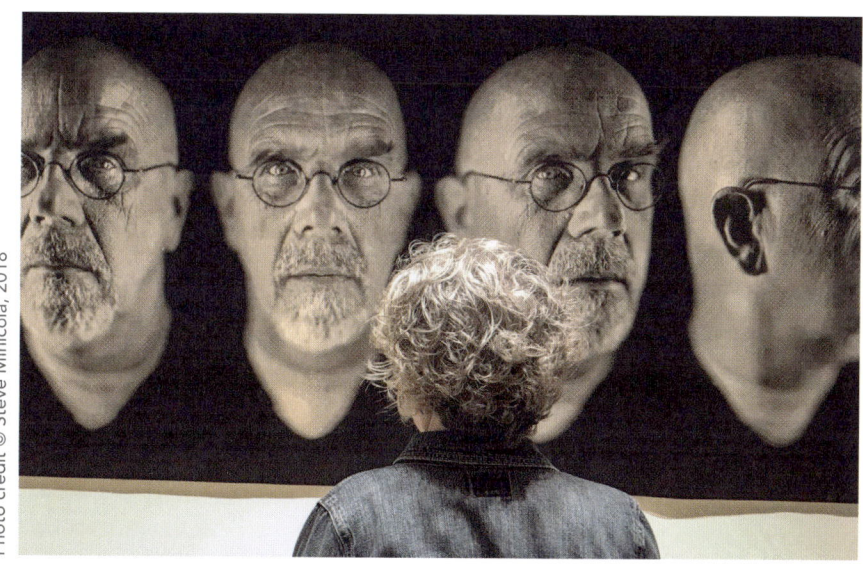

Photo credit © Steve Minicola, 2018

Installation view of *Chuck Close Photographs* at Philadelphia Academy of Fine Arts, Philadelphia, Pennsylvania, 2017.

But what if that visitor feels completely uncomfortable at the art exhibition? What if she feels completely intimidated by the art or by the crowd? An exhibition might be a second (or desired) home for an artist, but it can be an alienating experience for non-artists. Wall text can welcome visitors to the exhibition itself, providing information in a way that is familiar to many: in writing.

The best guide to exhibition standards for wall text is the *Smithsonian Guidelines for Accessible Exhibition Design* (SGAED), an excellent example of our US federal tax dollars at work.[3]

In short, it's hard to go wrong if SGAED's guidelines are followed. The SGAED is downloadable as a PDF and includes ADA-approved guidelines for exhibition content, works, installation standards, traffic, and so forth.

"Section B: Guidelines and Tools, Part III. Label Design and Text" recommends brief sentences that are written in plain English. Specialized jargon and technical language, for instance, are discouraged. As discussed in chapter 4, such rhetoric can alienate nonspecialists. If jargon and technical concerns are central to the objective of the exhibition, separate wall panels that describe the terms might be useful. An exhibition of sculpture that features the "lost wax technique," for instance, might benefit from introductory or supplementary wall panels that describe the technique for those who might be unfamiliar with the process. Or perhaps an event featuring work by an artist collective might benefit from a wall panel about the collective's history or objectives.

To achieve straight talk, SGAED recommends the following:

- Active voice

- 15–25-word limits per sentence

- 100-word limits per label

- 45–50 characters per line

These recommendations follow the same lines of reasoning made throughout this practical primer: write to communicate clearly and concisely. In the instance of wall text, plain talk can be even more important.

Those wall panels about exhibition objectives are like the stories told in Artist Statements. There are significant differences, though. Readers of stories told in Artist Statements have the luxuries of leisure and time. Readers of stories told in wall panels don't have either. Thus, SGAED's focus

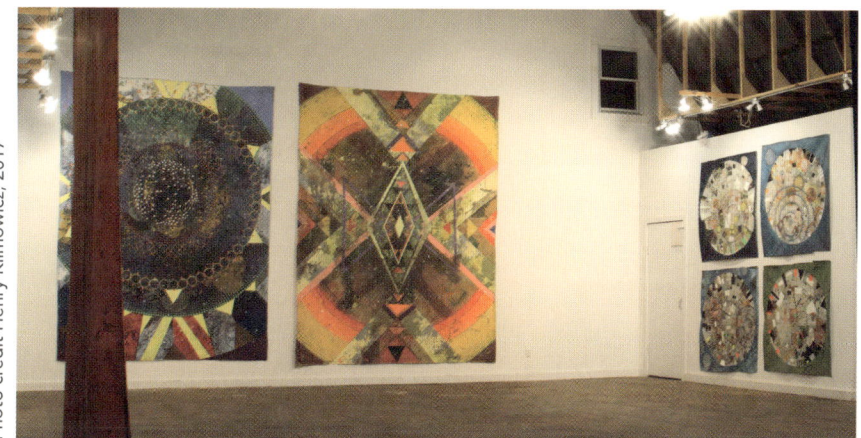

Jason Rohlf: Aeronauts & Oracles exhibition,
the Re Institute, Millerton, New York, 2016.

on lower word counts, all the while maintaining active voice, is right on target. The goal: to provide information that can be read and understood comfortably and quickly. Formal galleries and arts institutions usually have set standards for the wall text. In the case of independent installations, decisions about wall text usually fall to the exhibiting artist(s).

Keeping an eye on the readability of wall text, and keeping it from interfering with visibility, is a central guiding principle in any art installation. Note that SGAED recommends design standards that are based on legibility:

- Sans or simple serif typefaces

- Uppercase and lowercase letters in standard title or sentence format

- Type sizes relevant to installation heights

- Consistent spacing for letters and words

- Justified left margins

- High contrast between text and background

These standards help keep visibility from being taken for granted. Consistent spacing and installation heights of wall text are also guidelines worth observing. Consistency, it seems, appears to be an orienting principle throughout SGAED's recommendations.

The photo from Rochelle Weiner's *Strata+Sphere* exhibition at Café Lulu demonstrates such consistency. Note how she chose to write clear and readable standard wall labels featuring artist name, title of work, media, and size.

If there's so much 2-D art that the works need to be stacked, assigning numbers to works on particular gallery walls that correspond to numbers in explanatory handouts can work really well. The Re Institute's exhibition *Jason Rohlf: Aeronauts & Oracles* is a case in point. To identify the paintings—a mixture of large-scale and small acrylics on canvas or muslin works—the Re Institute provided a printed Object List with numbers corresponding to penciled numbers on the walls next to the paintings.

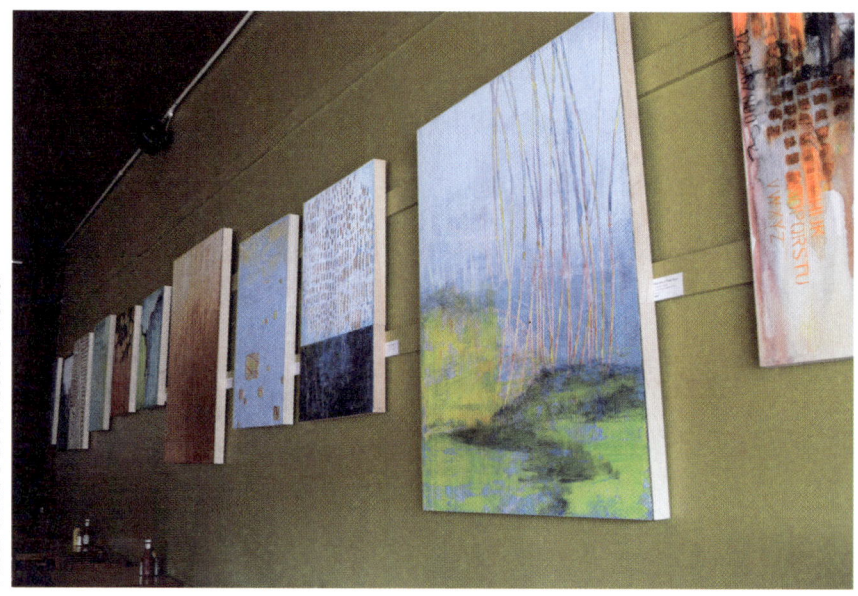

Installation view of Rochelle Weiner exhibition *Strata+Sphere*, Café Lulu, Milwaukee, Wisconsin, 2016.

In the installation view image from *Jason Rohlf: Aeronauts & Oracles*, for instance, the draped, large-scale painting suspended on the far left was numbered 70. Moving left to right, the next two panels were numbered 1 and 2. Moving on to the right wall pictured, the numbering continued left to right, top to bottom: the top-row acrylic/collages on canvas were thus numbered 3 and 4, while those on the bottom row were numbered 5 and 6. The penciled numbers on the wall were an efficient and elegant solution for this installation.

The Barnes Foundation (Philadelphia), renowned for its impressionist, postimpressionist, and early modern paintings, takes installation to an entirely new level. It forgoes wall text completely. Instead, it provides Collection Gallery Guides that use graphics like those for room 10 (see pp. 100–101) to identify the paintings, decorative arts, and historical artifacts. Artists, connoisseurs, enthusiasts, and historians nerd out at the Barnes, making bets about artist names and stages of artist careers before they turn to a Gallery Guide to settle their wagers.

The graphic maps for each Collection Gallery Guide are excellent visual aides. Room 10's south wall typifies installations at the Barnes: in addition to the stacked and symmetrically arranged canvases on the room walls, historical objects are also installed. In Barnes-speak, these installations are known as ensembles. They privilege visually dynamic experiences that foster conversation and understanding rather than art-historical standards such as genre or period. Wondering what paintings are represented by the gray blocks on the adjacent east and west walls of room 10? Maybe a trip to the Barnes is in order!

Clearly, there are a wide variety of techniques. The fun is to learn about installation processes and then about standards for identification—from the hallowed gallery walls of the Barnes to the familiar walls of coffee houses.

36

37

36 William James Glackens (American, 1870–1938).
    Then We All Went Home, 1909. Black crayon, charcoal,
    ink washes, and white gouache on wove paper. BF282

37 William James Glackens (American, 1870–1938).
    Beach with Figures, Bellport, c. 1915. Oil on canvas. BF175

Image © 2017 Barnes Foundation

Gallery Guide, room 10,
spread for south wall.
Designed by Pentagram
for the Barnes Foundation.

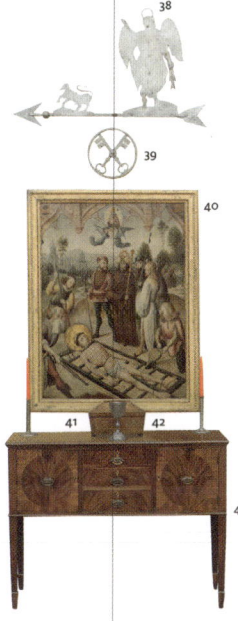

38

39

40

41 42

43

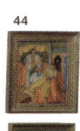

44

45

38 *Weather Vane*, probably 18th century. France.
    Iron. 01.02.31

39 *Gate Decoration*. Iron. 01.02.32

*40 Master of the Saint Ursula Legend and Workshop
    (German, active c. 1485–c. 1515). *Martyrdom of Saint
    Lawrence*, c. 1485/90–1510. Oil on canvas. BF265

41 *Box*, 19th century. Walnut veneer, metal, fabric, glass,
    and ivory. 01.02.34AD

42 *Chalice*, 1770–1780. Germany or United States.
    Pewter. 01.02.35

43 *Sideboard*, late 18th century. England. Mahogany, pine,
    oak, and brass. 01.02.40

    * *This attribution differs from that on the frame, reflecting
    current scholarship.*

44 Angelo Pinto (American, 1908–1994). *Two Figures*, 1933.
    Oil on canvas. BF1147

45 Karl Priebe (American, 1914–1976). *Miss Chalfont*, 1947.
    Casein on cardboard. BF1144

Writing Process into Practice

This chapter has covered a lot of ground. Those new to promotion and installation might feel a little overwhelmed. After a few experiences, though, the work becomes familiar, part of practice. And, yes, even fun.

➥ **6 / p. 155**

Since so much of the content is already (one hopes) part of studio practice, the timeline for broadcasting the word is fairly easy to observe.

Ideally, **four months prior to activity,** artists write down the following:

Title of activity

Details (who, what, when, where)

Description (what, why)

Confirmation (who / host or sponsor)

Three to four months prior to the activity, write and distribute the press release to monthly regional, shelter, and vanity publications. If high-resolution images are available, include them in the promotional packet. Much of the written content can be recycled for all print and online materials: the press release, invitations, announcements, and on-site support materials.

Two weeks prior to the event, distribute the press release and high-resolution images to daily newspapers.

Ten days prior to the event, distribute the press release and high-resolution images to daily newspapers and local radio and television stations.

Taken together, these promotional processes are part and parcel of studio practice. Scheduling time and resources for creating the work, deciding on a way to move the art work, meeting expenses, and following through with all promotional activities happen prior to any major arts activity.

After events, the artist website is a great place to archive events. Web pages such as "Press" or "Events" can record activities in reverse chronological order and serve as the artist's personal archive. Press Releases posted as PDFs or hotlinks to the host websites can be useful too.

ABOUT PAPER AND SCREENS

A quick note about writing for print versus writing for the web. For the most part, print is for readers while the internet is for scanners. If that foundational concept can be kept in mind, it will be easy to follow these guidelines:

- Visual hierarchies of scale prevail: put most important information first.

- White space is golden: using white space to divide portions of text or visuals increases readability.

- Brevity is the soul of readability: some experts recommend approximately 50 percent or less for content on the web.[4]

- Scanning for information rules: to increase readability, bulleted or numbered lists are recommended. Breaking up that white space with levels of headings—headings that are informative—can be useful as well.[5]

Note that awards, residencies, internships, public commissions, visiting appointments, and so forth are newsworthy events that deserve to be promoted as well. Writing and distributing Press Releases about such accomplishments helps keep the solitary achievements of the artist visible to an art-appreciating public.

Notes

1. See Holiday's *Growth Hacker Marketing* (2014).
2. Friedman, "'Eggs Benedict' Served at MAM" (2015), 6.
3. Smithsonian Guidelines for Accessible Exhibition Design (www.si.edu/Accessibility/SGAED), 17–26.
4. Nielsen's *Designing Web Usability* (1999).
5. Garrand's *Writing for Multimedia and the Web* (2001).

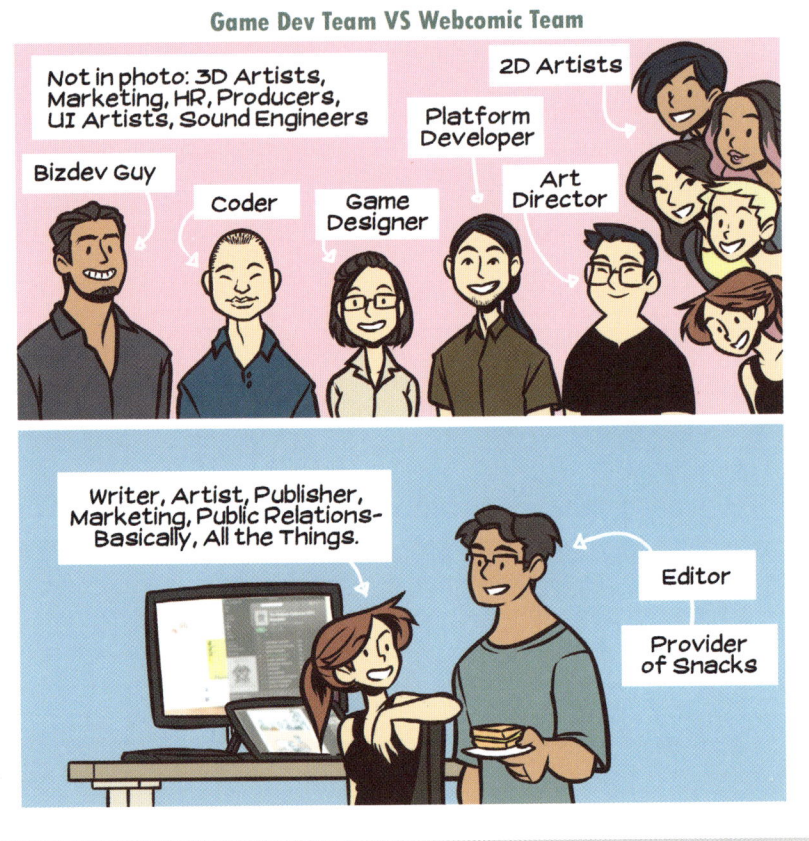

"Game Dev Team VS Webcomic Team." © 2017 Caroline Dy.
(Courtesy drawwriteplay.com.)

Conclusion:
Only the Individual Artist Can ___

Only the individual artist can bring creative and writing processes into studio practice; only the individual artist can decide which creative and writing processes deserve the most attention at any given time.

Establishing studio practice can be a fairly overwhelming experience for anyone. Much of the initial work involves establishing routine: hours in the studio as a maker, hours promoting work or participating in arts communities, hours researching opportunities, hours exhibiting work, hours making enough money to provide a studio as well as rent, food, clothing, and, well, life! And let's not forget all the new equipment and materials needed to establish and maintain a studio. That stuff's expensive.

The good news: writing doesn't cost anything, but it does take time. Dedicating a portion of studio practice to research and writing can fuel the promotion, participation, exhibition, and recognition of the work itself. This is an investment in practice that will pay off.

None of these processes or practices happen overnight. True, there are those who do indeed leap from art school into blue chip galleries. Such leaps tend to be the exception rather than the rule, though.[1] Unfortunately, there really aren't too many short cuts.

This primer began by introducing similarities between creative and writing processes, moved on to foundations in research and documentation, reinforced how the research and applied writing can become part of daily studio practice, and concluded with examples of event promotion.

Artists Write to Work sketches a commonsense path that leaves much room for detours and new directions. Take them. Explore! Just remember, to return to Mary Heilmann: it's all of a piece. Only the individual artist can know what her practice looks and feels like. The Farewell Forecasting Worksheet (p. 146) might help guide (or at least point) to new horizons to be explored. So get back to work!

Notes

1.   Davis, "How to Make It as an Artist in New York" (2016).

Appendix: Internet Resources

Education, government, and nonprofit internet resources referenced throughout *Artists Write to Work*, in alphabetical order. Websites active at time of publication.

American Alliance of Museums: www.aam-us.org
American Artist: www.americanartist.us
American Council of Learned Societies: www.acls.org
American Craft Council: https://craftcouncil.org
Americans for the Arts: www.americansforthearts.org
Art Fair Calendar: www.artfaircalendar.org
ARTinsight: www.artinsight.org
Barnes Foundation: www.barnesfoundation.org
Bureau of Labor Statistics: www.bls.gov
Call for Entry: www.callforentry.org
Canada Council for the Arts: http://canadacouncil.ca/
College Art Association: www.collegeart.org
Creative Capital: www.creativecapital.org
Duke Research Funding: http://researchfunding.duke.edu
Fractured Atlas: www.fracturedatlas.org
Fulbright Scholars: www.cies.org
Guide Star: www.guidestar.org
H-Net (Humanities Net): http://networks.h-net.org
National Center for Charitable Statistics: www.nccs.urban.org
National Endowment of the Arts: www.arts.gov/grants
National Endowment of the Humanities: www.neh.gov/grants
National Gallery of Art: www.nga.gov
National Parks Artist Residencies: www.nps.gov/subjects/arts
New York Foundation for the Arts: www.nyfa.org
Philanthropy News Digest: www.philanthropynewsdigest.org
Professional Artist Magazine: https://professionalartistmag.org
Schiffer Publishing: www.schifferbooks.com/artistswritetowork
ResArtis: www.resartis.org/en
US Government Grants: www.grants.gov

Key Terms

artist: Used interchangeably with *creatives* and *makers* throughout this book to reference independent creative professionals in visual and performing arts and design, broadly construed. *Working artists* and *independent artists*, those who make their living primarily through their craft, are used interchangeably as well.

Artist Biography: Brief narrative about the artist's personal background and professional training or interests.

Artist Resume: One-page record of artist background (such as awards, education, exhibitions).

Artist Statement: A story about artist's craft, experiences, goals, inspirations; typically related to particular events or exhibitions.

applied writing: Industry-specific practical writing strategies.

creative process: Individual elements and strategies related to creative production in an artist's medium; knowledge production.

critical analysis/writing: Writing informed by a wide range of historical, philosophical, or theoretical concepts.

formal analysis: Descriptive visual analysis that includes line, shape, color, organization of formal elements, media.

masters in fine arts (arts MFA): American standard bearer for terminal degree in studio art that requires creative production.

practice-based doctorates (arts PhDs): Australian and British standard bearer for terminal degree in studio art that requires critical writing component in addition to creative production.

studio practice: Standards and strategies that artists employ in their daily work.

writing process: Individual elements and strategies related to practical research and writing in support; knowledge production.

Case Studies

Fine Art Gallery Exhibition Promotion

Abel Contemporary Gallery (Paoli, Wisconsin)

Abel Contemporary Gallery owners Theresa Abel and Tim O'Neill have graciously shared promotional materials for a 2017 exhibition for this publication. AC Gallery has been a prominent leader in fine art and fine craft since 1998. Located between Madison, Wisconsin, and Chicago, Illinois, it has an excellent reputation built on representing highly regarded regional artists as well as those with national reputations.

In addition to promotional materials (a press release, advertisement, email invitation, and a postcard invitation), they shared an artist statement that began chapter 4 of this volume and that was included in the exhibition book *Of Eight Balls and Dictionaries* by painter Kelli Hoppmann. For Theresa, "Kelli's writing is a nice example of honest writing that is a reflection of her artwork and gives collectors an insight into who she is." To further promote Kelli's exhibition, Theresa wrote a short foreword to the exhibition book that was also used on the gallery's website blog (www.abelcontemporary.com). Here is an image of sample wall texts:

Theresa's foreword concludes the Case Study. Together, these materials represent cohesive, thorough, and engaging promotion of an exhibition as well as of a particular artist. If only every artist had such responsible and thoughtful representation in a career!

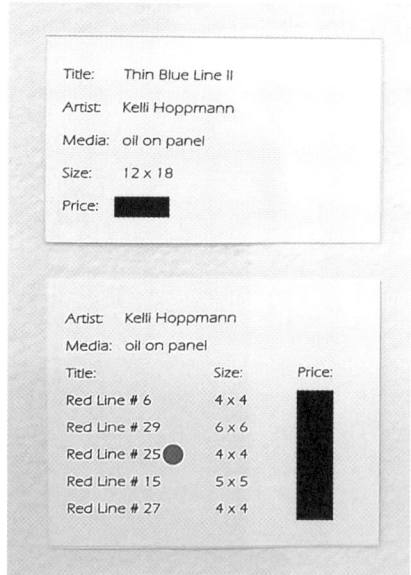

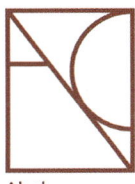

Abel
Contemporary
Gallery

News Release

For Immediate Release

Contact: Theresa Abel
6858 Paoli Rd.
Paoli, WI 53508
608-845-6600
Theresa@abelcontemporary.com
www.abelcontemporary.com

Abel Contemporary Gallery – announces three new exhibits

PAOLI, WI – 5/18/2017– **June 9th– July 23rd, 2017**
We present **Kelli Hoppmann: Dirt and the Clear Blue Sky; Group show: Thirty Artists for Thirty Years; and In the Cooler:** *Only Connect–* **Richard Jones**

Opening Reception Friday, June 9th , from 5pm-9pm. Open to the public.
Join us to celebrate 30 years of supporting the arts! Refreshments and live music by Five Points Jazz Collective.

Kelli Hoppmann: Dirt and the Clear Blue Sky
Madison artist, Kelli Hoppmann, has been painting about human weakness and strength for three decades. She has an endless curiosity of the world around her and can find inspiration in the familiar, draw drama from the ordinary, and see things that most of us overlook in our everyday lives. The figures in her allegories often don elaborate costumes, surrounded by lush environments; beautiful patterns and vivid color that make it hard to look away even when the topics might be challenging.

Thirty Artists for Thirty Years: Group show
Celebrating thirty years of supporting the arts, we have invited 30 of our artists to exhibit an outstanding piece for this singular show.

George Shipperley, Jonathan Wilde, Alicia Czechowski, Karen Halt, John Ribble, Mary Hood, S.V. Medaris, Kay Brathol-Hostvet, Deb Gottschalk, Chris Gargan, Ann Orlowski, Theresa Abel, Karl Borgeson, Allan Servoss, Greg Schulte, Ryan Myers, Paul Jeselskis, Joanne Kirkland, Jose Sierra, Gerit Grimm, Delores Fortuna, Rachelle Miller, Marlene Miller, Rick Hintze, Tim O'Neill, Scott Simmons, Richard Jones, Susan Richter-O'Connell, Yuyen Chang, Diane Washa

In the Cooler: *Only Connect–* Richard Jones
Only Connect will be the second installation in the gallery's cooler space for Madison artist, Richard Jones. Viewed from a distance, Jones will have erected a large wooden structure that upon closer inspection contains openings that reveal charred wooden blocks resembling a city no longer inhabited. Glass clouds illuminate the construction which is surrounded by framed drawings, maps, and other materials related to the natural world. It is up to the viewer to contemplate the connections that exist between these objects and relate them to their own experiences of the world.

Images included: Kelli Hoppmann – "Dirt and the Clear Blue Sky", Kelli Hoppmann – "The Hen House II", Richard Jones – "Only Connect", Ryan Myers – untitled sculpture, Gerit Grimm – "Mourners".

#

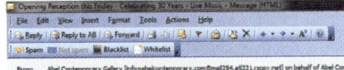

**Opening Reception this
Friday, June 9th, 5- 9 p.m.**

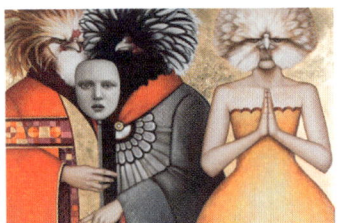

Hen House II - oil on panel

Opening reception for three new shows:
Kelli Hoppmann: *Dirt and the Clear Blue Sky*
Thirty Artists for Thirty Years: Group Show
In the Cooler:
Only Connect by Richard Jones

Join us for our 30th Anniversary Celebration

Five Points Jazz Collective

Friday, June 9th, 5-9 p.m.
Join us for the opening of these three exciting shows and our 30th Anniversary celebration.

Artist reception, refreshments, and live music by Five Points Jazz Collective.

Abel Contemporary Gallery
6858 Paoli Rd. Paoli, WI 53508

608-845-6600
www.AbelContemporary.com

Facebook   Website   Instagram

MailChimp

Abel Contemporary Gallery
Celebrating 30 Years

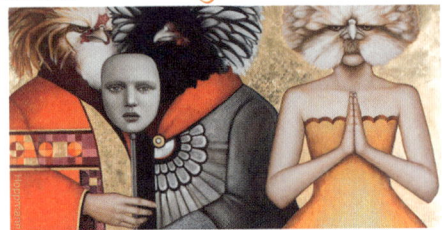

Join us to celebrate 30 years of fine art and fine craft.
Friday, June 9th, 5 - 9p.m.
Artist Reception, Live Music, Refreshments.

www.AbelContemporary.com
6858 Paoli Rd. Paoli, WI 53508 · 608-845-6600

Abel Contemporary Gallery
Celebrating 30 Years

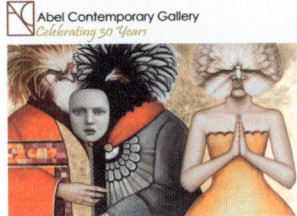

Dirt and The Clear Blue Sky - Kelli Hoppmann

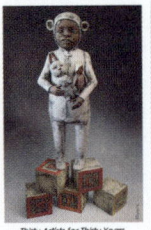

Thirty Artists for Thirty Years

Abel Contemporary Gallery
Located inside the creamery, Paoli, WI
6858 Paoli Rd. Belleville, WI 53508
Tuesday - Sunday 10:00 a.m. - 5:00 p.m.
AbelContemporary.com
608-845-6600

June 9th - July 23rd, 2017

Celebrating 30 Years
Friday, June 9th 5-9p.m.
Join us for the opening of these three exciting shows and our 30th Anniversary celebration.
Artist reception, refreshments, and live music by the Five Points Jazz Collective.

Kelli Hoppmann: *Dirt and the Clear Blue Sky* Madison artist, Kelli Hoppmann, has been painting about human strength and weakness for over three decades. The figures in her allegories often don elaborate costumes and are surrounded by lush environments. Beautiful patterns and vivid color draw you into these works and make it hard to look away, even when the themes might be challenging.
Group Show: *Thirty Artists for Thirty Years* To mark thirty years of fine art and fine craft in Paoli, WI, we have invited thirty of our gallery artists to exhibit an outstanding piece to celebrate this milestone event for the gallery.
In the Cooler: *Only Connect* by Richard Jones Jones fills the cooler with a large wooden structure reminiscent of a charred city, illuminated from above by glass clouds and surrounded by objects such as drawings, maps, and natural elements. It is up to the viewer to contemplate the connections that exist between these objects and relate them to their own experiences of the world.

Image: Jones

"Reflections on Knowing Kelli Hoppmann": Gallery Director Theresa Abel's Foreword to Exhibition Catalog

It is said that all artists are, throughout the length of their careers, basically painting the same painting over and over again. Kelli has been painting about human strength and weakness for over thirty years. Her themes of love, sin, politics, and redemption are repeated in paintings with titles such as *The Three Graces*, *Who Invited the Fascists?*, and *The Reluctant Anarchist*. Kelli is ever curious about what makes us human, and reminds us about what makes us animal.

I met Kelli while finishing an art degree at the University of Wisconsin–Madison. While we were both young painters, she was a few years my senior, and thus done with schooling, and figuring how to manage a life in the arts. With little money, neither of us had proper studios, but I learned from Kelli that it did not matter so much where you painted as long as you did it. She was always disciplined, painting or drawing more days than not, putting in at least four hours in her "studio" (read: closet) most days. She always made sure to find the time to get that much better, all while working a regular job to make sure she also got to eat.

Getting to know Kelli, I discovered she grew up in Madison, stayed on to receive a BFA in painting, then moved to New York City for a few years before returning to Madison, which is when I met her. For someone who has stayed so close to home, she has an endless curiosity of the world around her and is able to find inspiration in the familiar, draw drama from the ordinary, and see things that most of us overlook in our everyday lives.

Kelli brings the world to her through reading voraciously. Books are in piles around her home, and by looking at the varied titles we get some insight into her influences. The books in her home range from history books about Nazis to true crime, Buddhist tradition, biographies, philosophy, natural science, and, of course, the dictionary. While staying well read she manages to remain down to earth as ever, reading poetry after cheering on the Packers in football.

I've heard Kelli refer to herself as a frustrated writer or poet, and her paintings are poetic dramas played out in two dimensions, theatrical in their ability to create tension and narrative, while making the personal universal. The figures in her allegories often don elaborate costumes, surrounded by lush environments, beautiful patterns, and vivid color. Sometimes we get to live vicariously through these characters, attending fantasy parties, drinking too many martinis, smoking forbidden cigarettes, and all manner of poor decision making. These parties and other such tableaus seduce us into their world, making it hard to look away even when the topics might be challenging.

Anthropomorphism is one of her favorite devices to expose our animal nature. Innocents are rabbit prey to the devious fox predators; the clever are crows while the boorish become just that. Villains will be attired in as beautiful of costumes as the heroines and heroes of these dramas. The flatness of the panels that Kelli paints upon will often be reiterated with flat patterns and shallow depth of field that lends itself to the sense you are viewing a performance and the background is a stage set.

I've known Kelli for about as long as she's been a painter, and during that time the steady stream of work coming from her studio has been both impressive and, at times, hard to grasp. Even when she had two young children at home, she still managed to produce a notable amount of work. I've never known her to have a dry spell or creative block. Given that her influence is the entire world, this is not surprising. This book has been a wonderful chance to reflect on her career so far and has made me even more excited about where she will take her art in the years to come.

—Theresa Abel

Analysis of a Public Art Application

Utah Public Art Program & Department of Environmental Quality, Utah Division of Arts & Museums, Salt Lake City, Utah, June 2017

Public Art

Public art is most commonly associated with a sculpture or painting in areas accessible or visible to the public, but it goes well beyond those media. Terrazzo floors, etched glass, ceiling panels, textiles, stair railings, risers, pavers, planters, landscape, fences and grates are just some of the possibilities for public art contributions to public spaces. The possibilities are as vast as the imaginations of the artists and architects who create them.

Utah's Percent-for-Art Act

In 1985, the Legislature passed the Utah Percent-for-Art Act (Utah Code Title 9, Chapter 6, Sections 401-409), which designates 1% of construction costs of new and/or renovated state public buildings is added to the project for the purpose of commissioning, maintaining and conserving site specific art at, on, or in the facility. The collection includes a broad range of media from textiles and glass to stone and metal monumental works.

The Utah State Legislature Infrastructure and General Government Appropriations Subcommittee reviews all capital projects for the State and approves or cuts public art funding for those projects. If you would like to contact the legislators on the committee to express your views on art in public places, the committee membership and committee schedule and contact information can be found online.

Utah Public Art Program Opportunities

Utah Department of Environmental Quality
Letters of interest and qualifications are requested from artists interested in creating art for the public area(s) of the new Department of Environmental Quality Technical Support Center in Salt Lake City, Utah. The Selection Committee will collaborate with an artist to develop an installation that reflects the important role the Department of Environmental Quality plays in safeguarding Utah's air, land and water. The artist should consider that the Support Center is designed to help the Department ensure that all data collected is accurate, the science is reliable, and decisions are made based on the best available information. The Department also engages numerous stakeholders to participate in dialogue about environmental protection. The Committee encourages the artist to consider all of this, as does DEQ, in the spirit of service, protection, collaboration.
Applications are accepted via **CaFE** or digital copy (information / instructions available here.)
Budget: $40,500 – Deadline: June 30, 2017

The first section, "Public Art," gives general information about Utah's public art program. Its first paragraph draws broad strokes, *identifying possibilities as vast as the imaginations of the artists and architects who create them.* Its subsection is much more specific, detailing how the Utah legislature enacted a special code to allot a percentage of construction costs for the express purpose of *commissioning, maintaining, and conserving site-specific art.* The last subsection is even more broad, describing governmental oversight and responsibility.

The second section, "Utah Public Art Program Opportunities," introduces the specific project at the Utah Department of Environmental Quality (DEQ). A careful reading is instructive:

1. Requirements: Letter of Interest (LOI) and qualifications.

2. Key Phrase: *safeguarding Utah's air, land, and water.*

3. General goals of the project itself: ensure accuracy, scientific reliability, and access to information.

4. Key Concept: communication. Once selected, the process will be *collaborative*, with the selected artist and Selection Committee working together. DEQ seeks *dialogue about environmental protection* with its stakeholders.

5. Key Objective: *The Committee encourages the artist to consider all of this, as does DEQ, in the spirit of service, protection, collaboration.* This is a great note from the committee (representatives from the architectural firm Method Studio, Utah Facilities and Construction Management, DEQ, and Salt Lake County Public Art Program).[1]

Where did details about the Art Selection Committee come from? Page 5 of the DEQ's *Request for Artist Qualifications* guide (2017).[2]

This comprehensive guide deserves an analysis of its own. It repeats the DEQ's mission, *to protect the quality of our air, land and water*, as well as its dedication to communication, *work[ing] with individuals, community groups, and businesses* to fulfill its mission (p. 2). A closer read reveals the following:

1. location and site renderings of the building (*residential neighborhoods with views of mountains visible; 21,600 sq. ft; elevations and renderings appended to pamphlet*)

2. information about how the building functions, its purposes (*storage, active laboratories, and staging areas*)

3. inspiration for the architectural design (*from scientific nature of work, the effect of air and water upon the earth, to complement the residential neighborhood, and visibility*)

4. information about who will be using it (*field workers, scientists, storage personnel*)

5. concern for scale and visibility (within the neighborhood and from the perspective of the inhabitants of the building itself) taken by the architectural firm

6. construction materials (*durability*)

7. consideration of communication (*creating an inviting structure for staff, visitors, and the public*)

Taken together, these analyses reinforce the Key Phrase, Concepts, and Objectives noted in the announcement. The emphases on communication and collaboration are highlighted further by suggestions about specific site locations that would contribute to *public artwork /dialogue / engagement* (p. 3).

The remainder of the pamphlet details budget and acceptable expenses/reimbursements and gives submission options, instructions, and required materials. This section emphasizes the importance of following application instructions to the letter. On the one hand, it's restrictive: *Please do not include supplemental materials beyond the requirements listed below.* On the other hand, it's directive: *All applications must include the following* (p. 3).

It provides a number of specifications about the standard documents (resume, cover letter, images). The LOI, for instance, should not exceed three typewritten pages in PDF format. It needs to *include artist's reasons for interest in this project in particular.* The qualifications in the call specifically ask for a description about *how his/her work and/or experience relates to the project.* It also requests *six (6) images maximum of previous site-specific public work* (p. 4).

The enterprising applicant would need to think long and hard about whether his/her work would be appropriate for this project. The DEQ seems keen on an artist engaged in service to the community as well as to the environment, conservation and environmental concerns, and collaborative work (in development of the project as well as in the function of the installed work itself). Serve. Protect. Collaborate. These are the three key considerations. Tall orders, but an exciting project on the whole for the qualified candidate.

Notes

1. Utah's Public Art Program
    (https://heritage.utah.gov/arts-and-museums/public-art)
2. *Request for Artist Qualifications* (2017).

Worksheets

For printable format,
visit www.schifferbooks.com/artistswritetowork

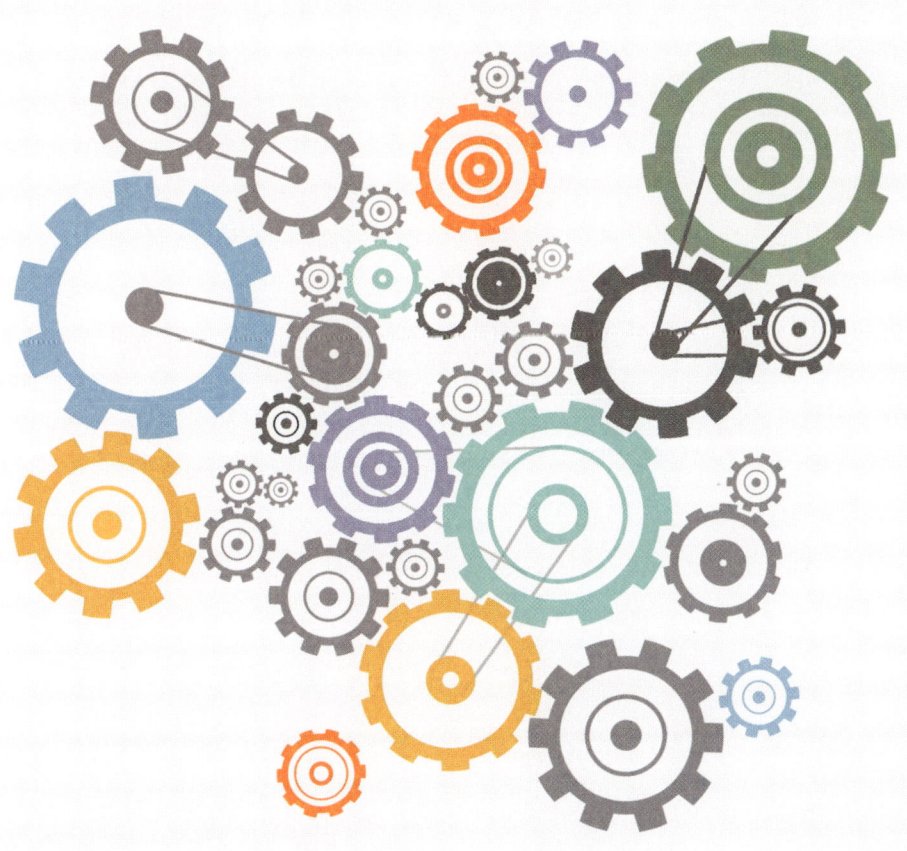

Writing Process || Creative Process

The parallels between the creative and writing processes will be returned to throughout *Artists Write to Work*. For now, take some time to think about creative processes and how they might parallel the writing processes.

1. What kind of research do you prefer?

Creative Processes ....

....

....

Writing Processes ....

....

....

2. Do you outline or sketch before beginning a project?

Creative Processes ....

....

....

....

Writing Processes ....

....

....

3. When working on a project, how many drafts or false starts do you make?

Creative Processes ....

....

....

Writing Processes ....

....

....

4. When working on a project, how many revisions do you do?

Creative Processes ....

....

....

Writing Processes ....

....

....

5. Does perfectionism stifle or promote your revision processes?

Creative Processes ....

....

....

Writing Processes ....

....

....

6. If you share your work with others for feedback or critique, how do you implement or respond to that feedback?

Creative Processes ....

....

....

....

Writing Processes ....

....

....

7. When do you know the work is "done"?

Creative Processes ....

....

....

Writing Processes ....

....

....

....

....

....

....

....

Doing the Homework

Arts Organizations

An electronic spreadsheet or a hard-copy table is a great way to record the research. In both cases, abbreviations in the columns can be useful, but they do mean someone needs to know what those abbreviations mean. For this worksheet, one key to abbreviations can serve both an electronic spreadsheet and a hard-copy table.

Key:

Institution	name of Institution
.org	nonprofit website
.com	commercial website
Contact	name of contact
Title	title of contact
Email	email address
Opps	exhibition or work opportunities
Events	public events

To create a workbook similar to the ARtSites_2017 sheet in chapter 2, try these steps:

1. Open Microsoft Excel

2. Select Blank Workbook

3. Save workbook

4. Make titles for each column

   Column A: Institution
   Column B: .org

   Column C: .com
   Column D: Contact
   Column E: Title
   Column F: Email
   Column G: Opps
   Column H: Events

5. Save workbook again

Then fill in the columns and save the sheet when complete.
Not up for a spreadsheet? Feel free to use the table shown here.

Institution ....

.org ....

.com ....

Contact ....

Title ....

Email ....

Opps ....

Institution ....

.org ....

.com ....

Contact ....

Title ....

Email ....

Opps ....

Doing the Homework

Commercial Art Galleries

By turning a critical eye to brick-and-mortar galleries, relevant and welcoming galleries will become self-evident.

Gallery Name

....

Address / City / State / Zip

....

....

....

Contact names and titles

....

....

Keywords: genres, media, period, size, neighborhood

....

....

....

Select Artists or Group of Artists

name ....

genre ....

media ....

date ....

price ....

Select Artists or Group of Artists

name ....

genre ....

media ....

date ....

price ....

Number of works on display in the gallery:

....

....

Method of installation:

....

....

NOTES:
What were the best parts of these visits?
What distinguished one gallery more than any of the others?

....

....

....

....

....

....

....

....

Taking Inventory

List of Accomplishments
(reverse chronology, most recent first)

Exhibitions

Date

Exhibition Title (solo/group)

Host/Sponsor

City ST

Solo/Group

Community Projects

Date

Community Project (collaborators)

Host/Sponsor

City ST

Other

Awards

Date

Award/Grant

Host/Sponsor

City ST

Other

Residencies

Date

Residency

Host/Sponsor

City ST

Other

Press Coverage

Date

Interviewer Name

Title of Program

Radio/TV station

City ST

Other

Education

Date

Degree

Name of Institution

City ST

Other

Internships

Date

Title

Name of Institution

City ST

Other

Add additional categories that relate to your work!

Taking Inventory

Anatomy of an Artist Resume
(with instructions in italics)

Section Header: HEADING, LETTERHEAD, OR LOGO

Name ....

Address / City, State ZIP ....

....

Phone number, email, website ....

....

Section Header: EDUCATION
Reverse chronology, most recent first

Institution, City, State ....

....

Degree (or anticipated degree) and date ....

Institution, City, State ....

....

Program and date ....

....

Section Header: AWARDS

Reverse chronology, most recent first

Award / Scholarship / Notice of Achievement and Date

Award / Scholarship / Notice of Achievement and Date

Section Header: RELATED WORK HISTORY

Reverse chronology, most recent first

Job Title / Institution Name, City, State / Date

Job Title / Institution Name, City, State / Date

Section Header: EXHIBITION HISTORY

Reverse chronology, most recent first

Subsection Header: Solo

"Title of Show," Gallery or Host Organization Name, City, State / Year

Subsection Header: Group

"Title of Show," Gallery or Host Organization Name, City, State / Year

Subsection Header: Juried

Telling the Story

An Inventory

These questions are designed to jump-start the brainstorming process. Hopefully, they will help promote connections that might otherwise escape notice.

Introduce Yourself

What's your name? / What are your nicknames?

Where do you live? Study?

Where else have you lived?

Where do you want to live?

Other

Media

What is your preferred media?

Why?

What other media do you enjoy or would like to learn more about?

Other

Tools

What tools do you need?

....

What tools do you like?

....

What tools do you invent?

....

Do you have ready access to these tools? Why ∕why not?

....

Genre

Portraiture? ....

Landscape? ....

Environmental ∕ Land Art? ....

Installation? ....

Combination of genres? ....

Other? ....

Style

Abstraction ....

Realism ....

Miniature ....

Photorealism ....

Landscape ....

Digital ....

Installation ....

Other ....

Practice: Time

Time of Day/Night ....

Times a Week (Sporadic schedule? Regulated schedule?) ....

Duration ....

Practice: Environment

Location/Size ....

Solitary? Shared? Collaborative? ....

Spatial Organization

(*Mise en place*? Chaos? Something in between?) ....

Silence? Music?

....

Key Moments
(Write on a separate page or journal)

Past ....

Current ....

Anticipated ....

Frustrations

(Write on a separate page or journal)

Celebrations

Professional ....

Personal ....

Career Level ....

Student ....

Emerging ....

Midcareer ....

Jobs

(Use space below or write on a separate page or journal)

....

....

....

Strengths & Weaknesses

Formal Analysis ....

Stylistic Analysis ....

Theoretical Analysis ....

....

....

Influences
(Use space below or write on a separate page or journal)

Art-Historical

....

....

Personal

....

....

Theoretical

....

....

Cultural

....

....

Other
Interests (Use space below or write on a separate page or journal)

Hobbies, Food, Sports

....

....

Other Media

....

....

Other Artistic Endeavors

....

....

....

Other Scholarly Disciplines

....

....

....

....

Other Work

....

....

....

....

....

....

....

....

....

Aspirations
(Write on a separate page or journal)

Curiosity
(Write on a separate page or journal)

Confidence
(Write on a separate page or journal)

Other
(Write on a separate page or journal)

Applying Yourself

Priorities

This worksheet is designed to help an artist be analytically introspective. What does the artist what to achieve? What steps might be taken to achieve stated goals? How might the goals for a project align with those of a specific opportunity (program, school, grant, fellowship, residency)? If the project and the opportunity don't quite seem to match, it might be a good time to reconsider priorities or to continue to search for an opportunity more aligned with the project.

What do you want to accomplish?

How will the artist's project contribute to the field?

What resources will support the project?

What is a reasonable timeline?

Is it enough time to complete the project?

How will the project's success be gauged?

What is the mission of the host/sponsor?

What are the objectives for the host/sponsor opportunity?

How does the project relate to the mission or the opportunity?

Applying Yourself

Research

Once that opportunity aligned with an artist's project is found, it's time to research information about the institution.

What patterns (if any) exist in the awards?

Who are recipients? What are the amounts of awards?

What does the IRS 990 (www.guidestar.org/Home.aspx) reveal about trends in awards?

Who's in charge? What's their history?

What does the press on the site reveal?

What does a general press search reveal?

What do the institution's publications represent?

Who serves on the board or committee?

Are instructional webinars scheduled? If so, when?

Who are the appropriate contacts?

Applying Yourself

Analysis

After completing the Priorities and Research Worksheets, the enterprising artist is ready to give the sponsoring institution's website content a thorough analysis. The data collected in this worksheet will be useful when it comes time to write the cover letter or project statement.

Keywords

Which of these keywords relate to proposed project?

Verb tense (sample sentences)

Vocabulary (samples)

Method of address (familiar? reserved?)

....

....

Number of sentences per paragraph

....

....

Number of paragraphs per page

....

....

Use of visuals

....

....

Use of white space

....

....

....

....

....

Broadcasting the Word

Anatomy of a Press Release

Letterhead or Artist Address

Contact

Date

Banner: News Headline

Blurb Paragraph: Explanation of Headline

Paragraph 1: Snapshot of Details

Paragraph 2: Significance of Event

Paragraph 3: Support for Significance of Event

....

....

Paragraph 4: Closing paragraph complete with particulars (address, open hours) and host institution tagline (standard statement that accompanies all host publicity)

....

....

....

....

....

....

....

: The hashtags signify end of document

CONCLUSION

Farewell Forecasting

Use the spaces provided or (better yet!)
write it all down in a journal.

What's the situation at present?

What are the short-term goals? (next six to twelve months)

What are the goals for next year?

What does three years from now look like?

What does five years from now look like?

What does seven to ten years from now look like?

What steps can be taken to support these goals?

➲ **GuideNotes** for Educators

Many thanks to Julie Mikolajewski and Tiffany Settles, who graciously reviewed these GuideNotes and made excellent suggestions for expanding lessons. Both women teach at Sadie Tanner Mossell Alexander University of Pennsylvania Partnership School (West Philadelphia, Pennsylvania).

Introduction

Teaching artists work around the clock, either in the classroom or in the studio. Unfortunately, classroom demands seem to take precedence over creative practice more often than not for American teachers, as countless reports by the the likes of the National Endowment for the Arts, National Art Education Association, and National Association of Schools of Art and Design attest. It's also pretty well established that the arts curriculum is overcrowded (see Houghton 2016). Add local, state, and federal mandates in the United States or provincial standards in Canada into the mix, and the overcrowded curriculum becomes standing room only!

Thus, GuideNotes are designed in general to make it easier to integrate writing into your existing visual arts curriculum—whatever grade you teach, wherever you live. They are not (repeat, not!) lesson plans: that's your wheelhouse, not mine. Instead, they reference activities aligned with American Common Core English Language Arts standards (CCS.ELA), such as strategic integration of media and other written texts, careful readings of textual evidence, identification of how words shape meaning or tone, collaborative work, written arguments focused on discipline-specific content, clearly written explanatory texts, research, and presentation of knowledge. The activities, intentionally broad, can be scaled up for higher grades or down for the littles and can be adapted to a variety of resources. May your students have fun when they express their own art experiences in writing!

➲ 1. Journaling

Journaling, for artists, is familiar ground. Expanding journaling to include guided writing in the classroom is just adding another layer to the practice itself, a layer that facilitates critical self-awareness and metacognitive reflection (see Marshall 2014). Writing in journals offers another important learning strategy: practice. Integrating the writing on an iterative, regular basis can be as simple as students reflecting upon the day's work in daily written entries. For the purposes of these GuideNotes, using a journal as a graphic organizer and sketchbook is understood as central to the writing process.

After examining their journals to see which concepts and vocabulary words recur, students can make confident, informed decisions about how to describe and share their visualizations in presentations. Maybe a particular student returns to a particular metaphor; if so, maybe she can synthesize across her journal entries to develop a summary metaphor about her perceptions or her work. It's a win-win. With practice, the journaling itself can become a habit of mind.

Added bonus: journaling helps teachers track student progress, follow knowledge transfer across disciplines, and forecast future lesson plans.

The Common Core Standard for English Language Standard Range of Writing seems to be the most relevant standard (CCS.ELA W8.10) for ongoing journal writing:

> Write routinely over extended time frames (time for reflection and revision) and shorter time frames (a single sitting or a day or two) for a range of discipline-specific tasks, purposes, and audiences). *See www.corestandards. org/ELA-Literacy/CCRA/W*

Consistent journal writing encourages creative thinking and its implementation, problem solving and reasoning, and clear communication. It also provides an independent space to develop intellectual curiosity and flexibility (particularly as the latter relates to processing feedback), time management, and work habits. Who knew that the age-old practice of keeping a daily journal would be so remarkably suited for the US Framework for 21st Century Learning?

➲ 2. Field Trips as Text

Field trips provide excellent opportunities for student engagement with fine art, community, and cultural centers. They also provide excellent opportunities to see how students experience a place they've visited. Asking students to engage with the site of the field trip destination can reenergize traditional queries about the art, science, or social impact of a particular place.

In terms of current American education standards, students can activate prior knowledge about such activities, research the field trip destination online, and then compare and contrast this information with the print materials distributed at the site. Students (working in pairs) could examine connotation and denotation of words, phrases, and images as they appear online and in printed materials available at the site; write a presentation; present their findings; and then reflect upon the whole experience in their journals. The prompts in the Commercial Art Galleries worksheet for chapter 2, "Doing the Homework" (p. 124) can be modified to reflect particular field trip objectives (CCS.ELA R1.4, R1.6, R7, SL5, W7, W8.10).

Other activities could involve descriptions of the buildings or site visited. These could range anywhere from first impressions to art-historical analyses, complete with sketches of the buildings themselves. Integration of ELA, History, and Math standards could relate to these activities. Finally, Julie Mikolajewski suggested a "Roaming Docent" assignment: students could choose an object or two at the visited site, write an informational text about the object(s), and then return to the object(s) to verbally share that text with visitors to the site (CCS.ELA SL 12.4).

➲ 2.1. The Stories Websites Tell

Websites are great storytellers. Putting the written content of an art organization's home page under the microscope seems like a logical way to extend analyses of written and visual rhetoric. Such an exercise could involve the evaluation of accuracy, credibility, and readability. A longer research project could focus on analyses of the multiple levels of meaning and tone represented on any given website. Students could be divided into groups or pairs to analyze text-based and visual content before presenting their analyses of the technical, connotative, denotative, and figurative elements. Student journaling could include note taking, keyword identification (and definition), and rhetorical analyses of written and visual content (CCS. ELA R7, SL5, W7, W8.10).

Looking for a shorter research project? Ask students to identify a website's controlling idea. Then ask them (in groups or in pairs) to trace how the controlling idea is developed throughout the website and then to present the findings to the class (CCS.ELA R1, R1.2, R7, SL5, W7 + R1.4).

Tiffany Settles was enthusiastic about students creating a website art portfolio for a particular project or class. She also saw the project as an opportunity to collaborate with other faculty. This collaborative, ongoing project would involve multiple skill sets. Please see GuideNote "The Big, REALLY BIG, Picture" for chapter 6 (p. 151). It spells out the connections to 21st Century Learning skills such as critical thinking, collaboration, clear communication, adaptability, effective interaction with others, project management, and information, media, and Information, Communication, Technology (ICT) literacies. It also addresses the Math, Reading, Research, Technology, and Writing Standards that would be met as well.

➲ 3. Artist Resume and Artist Biography

Chapter 3's worksheets (pp. 127 to 131) would be most relevant to seniors in high school and students pursuing postsecondary art education. After all, they'll be needing Artist Resumes and Artist Biographies sooner than later! Writing a one-page resume based on a renowned contemporary artist's career would be an effective exercise in genre (resume) and research (CCS.ELA R1, R7, SL5, W7).

Want to introduce another creative element? After students have done the research and written the resume, ask students to write a narrative pretending that they are that renowned contemporary artist. Ask them to use imagery and sensory language to develop their work (CCS.ELA R7, SL5, W7 + W8.3).

The Framework for 21st Century Learning skills demonstrated in chapter 3 include critical thinking, literacy in clear communication, project management, and information, media, and ICT. Student journaling could be a place for writing notes or sketches about their research and for drafting these support documents (CCS.ELA 8.10).

➲ 4. Telling Stories

Analysis of Artist Statements is the mother lode when it comes to students developing understandings about discipline-specific activities, objectives, and audiences. For instance, ask students to compare two different Artist Statements from two mature artists who work in the same genre but are represented by two different organizations.

For example, American artists Kerry James Marshall and Kara Walker both are known for their explorations of race and identity. Analyses of the textual representation of their work would extend beyond the formal elements of their artworks to a range of social issues such as family, gender, and sexuality. Both artists have received the coveted MacArthur Fellowship and have been featured on Art21. Marshall is currently represented by Jack Shnaiman Gallery (www.jackshainman.com/artists/kerryjames-marshall), while Sikemma Jenkins & Co. represent Walker (www.sikkemajenkinsco.com/kara-walker). Students can compare diction, syntax, and rhetorical strategies of the artists (Kara Walker has her own website) as well as of the galleries that represent them, the museums that feature their work, or the narratives told in the televised program Art21 (CCS.ELA R1, R1.2, R4, R6, R7, SL2, SL5, W7, W8.1, W8.2, W8.4, W8.7–W8.9).

The research and analysis of Artist Statements, such as those for the Artist Resume and Artist Biography, also provide an excellent platform for writing narratives that develop through sophisticated use of imagery and sensory language. Narratives could be wall texts, short stories, or children's picture books about artists. For standards related to wall texts, commonly referred to as tombstones in museum work, please see chapter 6 (p. 186) or the *Smithsonian Guidelines for Exhibition Design* (www.si.edu/Accessibility/SGAED) (CCS.ELA R1, R1.2, R7, SL5, W7 + W8.3).

➲ 4.1. Everything Has a Place

Questions about the visual impact of an individual home page and the stories it tells are probably endless. In terms of learning about craft and structure, analyzing, and then comparing websites of two different arts organizations that serve widely different audiences, such as MASS MoCA (www.massmoca.org) and Wadsworth Atheneum Museum of Art (www.thewadsworth.com), referenced in chapter 4 (p. 70), would broaden interpretations of written and visual rhetoric. Younger students might be more interested in comparing institutions that relate directly to them: children's museums (such as Philadelphia's Please Touch Museum [www.pleasetouchmuseum.org] and the Franklin Institute [www.fi.edu]). Group presentations on the technical, connotative, and figurative meanings derived from the analyses would contribute to student understandings about how levels of meaning and tone reflect the identities of the individual arts organizations (CCS.ELA R1, R1.2, R4, R7, R10, SL1, SL5, W1.A–E, W7).

➲ 5. Taking the Leap

Whether on the walls outside a classroom, in the gym, or in a gallery, student art exhibitions and awards occur on a regular basis. In lower and middle school, the showcased artwork often corresponds to topics or readings in social studies or literacy. These are great opportunities for teachers to collaborate on making connections across the curriculum by sharing vocabulary, for instance, and that's great! In high school and beyond, getting students to take the leap beyond standard exhibitions can be like pulling teeth, but encouraging them to apply for juried exhibitions is worthwhile. The task, of course, is to keep an eye out for exhibitions that allow student submissions such as the 2018 SCWS (South Carolina Watermedia Society) Spring Digital Show.

Websites such as CaFÉ (www.callforentry.org) offer categories such as Youth and Award as well as Fee or No Fee to refine searches on the site. Want to put it all in the hands of the students? They can become members, create profiles, choose the most relevant categories, and then receive regular emails from CaFÉ about new opportunities.

Of course, all this sounds great until the deadline approaches. Student presentations on the application and exhibition experiences would relate to a variety of standards, but mainly CCS.ELA SL12.4 and SL 12.5. After a successful exhibition, there's one more step: updating the resume (see chapter 3). Like the artist's support documents (Biography, Resume, Statement), the application process certainly prepares students for college and real-world responsibilities.

Another, more developed assignment to promote student engagement would be researching and writing applications for arts programs, graduate schools, and grants. The Research and Analysis Worksheets for chapter 5, "Applying Yourself" (pp. 138–143), can be modified to reflect particular educational and funding objectives (CCS.ELA R1, R1.2, R7, SL5, W7).

2018 SCWS SPRING DIGITAL SHOW

Requirements

Media Images: Minimum, 1; Maximum, 1

Total Media: Minimum, 1; Maximum: 1

Entry Fee (SCWS Member Entry Fee): $25.00

Entry Fee (Student Entry Fee): $5.00

The South Carolina Watermedia Society (SCWS) calls for entry into its Spring Members Digital Show and Inaugural Student Digital Show.

Eligibility

The competition is open to any member whose dues are current. Dues run from January 1 to December 30. Dues can be paid when entering the show. Membership is open to adults 18 or older.

The Student show is open to any South Carolina students ages 13–17.

All work submitted must be the sole work of the entering artists. All water-soluble media, except water-soluble oils. Where collage is used, it should be less than 50 percent of the image. Images painted from published sources or completed under instruction in a class or workshop are not acceptable. Work should have been created no later than 2015.

Dates

Entries accepted from February 25, 2018, and close April 27, 2018
Awards winners will be notified via email.
www.callforentry.org/festivals_unique_info.php?ID=5169

➲ **6.** The Big, REALLY BIG, Picture

Organizing and installing those annual (and semiannual) student art exhibitions provides excellent opportunities for student collaboration and for art teachers to involve interested faculty. With teacher guidance, such activities would involve a range of disciplines and levels of knowledge and skill. For instance, an initial classroom discussion about the elements involved in an exhibition might yield the following:

1. Number of participating artists

2. Number of works per artist

3. Date of exhibition opening

4. Time needed to install exhibition

5. Space for exhibition

6. Method of installation

7. Installation materials needed

8. Title and description of exhibition

9. Number of invitations

10. Wall text?

11. Wall labels?

12. Method of invitation distribution

13. Press Release

14. Reception?

15. Reception food and beverage?

16. Who's going to pay for all of this?

Once all these elements are up on the whiteboard or chalkboard, discussion can turn to the division of labor:

1. Installation Crew

Establish installation timeline / determine artwork installation methods / specify staging materials / create installation supply list

CCS Math; Technology; Research; Collaboration

2. Promotional Crew

Share promotion timeline with design crew / develop press list / write and distribute press release / write wall text content / write invitation content / write list of works

CCS Writing; Research

3. Design Crew

Share promotion timeline with promotional crew / graphic design of wall text / graphic design of invitation / graphic design of list of works / research estimates for invitation printing and share with coordinating team

CCS Math; Technology; Research

4. Event Crew

Determine number of guests for reception / write letters to request funding for exhibition and reception materials / share reception activities with coordinating team

Math; Writing; Research

5. Coordinating Team

Primary hub for communications between crews / develop budget / authorize purchases / coordinate activities between crews / maintain schedule

Math; Writing; Collaboration

Add Tiffany Settles's idea for a website portfolio about an art class's accomplishments (see GuideNote 2.1, p. 151), and you have a professional-level art exhibition envisioned, organized, and realized by students. For lower-grade school students, the entire project could be scaled down, or focusing on one or two elements would do the trick. With guidance, this activity is probably most relevant to high school and college students, although middle schoolers could probably pull it off, too. And the steps involved are probably familiar to any of the students involved in dance, music, and theater performances. Bring in Julie Mikolajewski's idea about student presentations on areas of particular interest to them, or maybe an all-class presentation at the exhibition opening before students take their stations, and the Big, REALLY Big, Picture is complete (CCS.ELA 12.1A–12.1D, 12.2, 12.4, 12.6).

Bibliography

Alam, Murad, Karen C. Barrett, Robert M. Hodapp, and Kenneth A. Arndt. 2008. "Botulinum Toxin and the Facial Feedback Hypothesis: Can Looking Better Make You Feel Happier?" *Journal of the American Academy of Dermatology* 58 (6): 1061–72.

Andrelchik, Hillary. 2015. "Reconsidering Literacy in the Art Classroom." *Art Education* 65:6–11.

Apps, Linda, and Carolyn Mamchur. 2009. "Artful Language: Academic Writing for the Art Student." *International Journal of Art and Design Education* 28 (3): 269–78.

Artybollocks Generator. www.artybollocks.com/.

Barnet, Sylvan. 2011. *A Short Guide to Writing about Art*. 10th ed. New York: Pearson, 2011.

Barrett, Estelle, and Barbara Bolt, eds. 2007. *Practice as Research: Approaches to Creative Arts Inquiry*. London: I. B. Tauris.

Battenfield, Jackie. 2009. *The Artist's Guide: How to Make a Living Doing What You Love*. Philadelphia: Da Capo.

Beckman, Gary D. 2007. "'Adventuring' Arts Entrepreneurship Curricula in Higher Education." *Journal of Arts Management, Law, and Society* 37 (2): 25.

Bhandari, Heather Darcy, and Jonathan Melber. 2009. *Art/Work: Everything You Need to Know (and Do) as You Pursue Your Art Career*. New York: Free Press.

Bridgstock, Ruth. 2013. "Professional Capabilities for Twenty-First Century Creative Careers: Lessons from Outstandingly Successful Australian Artists and Designers." *JADE (International Journal of Art and Design Education)* 32 (2): 176–89.

Bureau of Labor Statistics. United States Department of Labor. www.bls.gov/ooh/arts-and-design/craft-and-fine-artists.htm#tab-2, accessed May 23, 2017.

Candlin, Fiona. 2000. "Practice-Based Doctorates and Questions of Academic Legitimacy." *JADE (International Journal of Art and Design Education)* 19 (1): 96–101.

———. 2001. "A Dual Inheritance: The Politics of Educational Reform and PhDs in Art and Design." *JADE (International Journal of Art and Design Education)* 20 (3): 302–10.

Caplin, Lee. 1998. *The Business of Art*. 3rd ed. Paramus, NJ: Prentice Hall.

Cheng, Woong Jo, and Margaret Wyszomirski. 2015. "What Is Arts Entrepreneurship? Tracking the Development of Its Definition in Scholarly Journals." *Artivate: Journal of Entrepreneurship in the Arts* 4 (2): 11–31.

Childers, Pamela B., Eric H. Hobson, and Joan A. Mullin, eds. 1998. *ARTiculating: Teaching Writing in a Visual World*. Portsmouth NH: Boynton/Cook.

College Art Association Standards and Guidelines. http://collegeart.org/guidelines/resume.

Collinson, Jacquelyn Allen. 2005. "Artistry and Analysis: Student Experiences of UK Practice-Based Doctorates in Art and Design." *International Journal of Qualitative Studies in Education* 18 (6): 713–28.

Congdon, Lisa. 2014. *Art Inc.: The Essential Guide for Building Your Career as an Artist*. San Francisco: Chronicle Books.

D'Alleva, Anne. 2004. *Look! The Fundamentals of Art History*. Upper Saddle River, NJ: Prentice Hall.

Daniels, Lawrence J. 2013. *The Graphic Designer's Business Survival Guide*. New York: American Management Association.

Davis, Noah. 2016. "How to Make It as an Artist in New York." *Crain's New York Business* 32 (12): 15. EBSCO MegaFILE, EBSCOhost, accessed April 5, 2017.

Donahue, David M., and Jennifer Stuart, eds. 2010. *Artful Teaching: Integrating the Arts for Understanding across the Curriculum, K–8*. New York: Teachers College Press.

Dunn, Rita, Jeffrey S. Beaudry, and Angela Klavas. 1989. "Survey of Research on Learning Styles." *Educational Leadership* 46 (6): 50–59.

Friedman, Tyler. 2015. "'Eggs Benedict' Served at MAM." *Shepherd Express*, August 18.

Garrand, Timothy. 2001. *Writing for Multimedia on the Web*. 2nd ed. Woburn, MA: Focal Press.

Goddard, Stephen. 2007. "A Correspondence between Practices." In *Practice as Research: Approaches to Creative Arts Enquiry*. Edited by Estelle Barrett and Barbara Bolt, 113–21. London: I. B. Tauris.

Grant, Daniel. 2010. *The Business of Being an Artist*. 4th ed. New York: Allworth.

Halliday, Christina. 2005. "'I Came to Art School So I Wouldn't Have to Write . . .': Creating New Contexts for Critical Writing in Post-secondary Art and Design Education." *Language and Literacy* 7 (1), www.langandlit.ualberta.ca.

Heilmann, Mary. 2011. "Obsessive-Compulsive Daydreaming." *Art Journal* 70 (2): 42–49.

———. Videos, https://art21.org/artist/mary-heilmann/.

Hemmig, William S. 2008. "The Information-Seeking Behavior of Visual Artists: A Literature Review." *Journal of Documentation* 64 (3): 343–62.

Hjelde, Katrine. 2015. "Paradox and Potential: Fine Art Employability and Enterprise Perspectives." *Art, Design & Communication in Higher Education* 14 (2): 175–88.

Holiday, Ryan. 2014. *Growth Hacker Marketing*. New York: Penguin.

Houghton, Nicholas. 2016. "Six into One: The Contradictory Art Curriculum and How It Came About." *JADE (International Journal of Art and Design Education)* 35.1: 107–20.

Johnson, Kim, Jennifer Yurchisicin, and Denise Bean. 2003. "The Use of Writing in the Apparel Curriculum: A Preliminary Investigation." *Clothing and Textiles Research Journal* 21 (1): 41–48.

Kansas Department of Commerce. www.kansascommerce.com/caic, accessed October 24, 2014.

Kleon, Austin. 2012. *Steal Like an Artist: 10 Things Nobody Told You about Being Creative*. New York: Workman.

Kruger, Barbara. 2002. Interview. EGG, *The Arts Show*, PBS, www.pbs.org/wnet/egg/217/kruger/interview_content_1.html, accessed June 15, 2014.

Lerner, Ruby. September 2016. "The Art School of the Future." In *Creativity Connects: Trends and Conditions Affecting U.S. Artists*. By Center for Cultural Innovation for Endowment for the Arts, 57. Washington, DC: National Endowment for the Arts.

Marshall, Julia. 2014. "Curriculum and Arts Integration as an Agency of Change." *Visual Inquiry: Learning and Teaching Art* 3 (3): 361–76.

Mueller, Pam A., and Daniel M. Openheimer. 2014. "The Pen Is Mightier Than the Keyboard." *Psychological Science* 25 (6): 1159–1168.

Nguyen, Thai. 2015. "10 Surprising Benefits You'll Get from Keeping a Journal." *The Blog*, February 13, www.huffingtonpost.com/thai-nguyen/benefits-of-journaling-_b_6648884.html.

Nielsen, Jakob. 1999. *Designing Web Usability: The Practice of Simplicity*. Indianapolis, IN: New Riders.

Paltridge, Brian, Sue Starfield, Louis Ravelli, and Sarah Nicholson. 2012. "Doctoral Writing in the Visual and Performing Arts: Two Ends of a Continuum." *Studies in Higher Education* 37 (8): 989–1003.

Paper Monument, ed. 2012. *Draw It with Your Eyes Closed: The Art of the Art Assignment*. Brooklyn, NY: Paper Monument.

Parkinson, Gavin. 2011. "(Blind Summit) Art Writing, Narrative, Middle Voice." *Art History* 34 (2): 268–87.

Pinker, Steven. 2014. "Why Academics Stink at Writing." *Chronicle of Higher Education*, September 26: 4–10.

ProbCause, animation, script, and performance. *How to Graduate from Art School* (animation), 1 hour, 30 minutes, www.youtube.com/watch?v=T8R@7_dsW5Y, published November 18, 2013.

Rappaport, Mat. Fall 2013. "Project 3: VisualPoetic [*sic*] Assignment." Motion Graphics 1, Columbia College (Chicago, IL).

Ricci, Mike. 2007. "Making a Statement: How and Why to Create an Effective Artist's Statement." *Craft's Report*, 14–16.

Robinson, Anne. 2009. "Underwriting: An Experiment in Charting Studio Practice." *Journal of Visual Arts Practice* 8 (1–2): 59–74; 70.

Rolling, J. H., Jr. 2013. *Arts-Based Research Primer*. New York: Peter Lang.

Salazar, Stacey. 2016. "A Portrait of the Artists as Young Adults: A Longitudinal Study of Art College Graduates." *Art, Design & Communication in Higher Education* 15 (2): 145–49.

Schjeldahl, Peter. 1998. "A Gang Theory of Art Education, or Why Artists Make the Worst Students." *Chronicle of Higher Education*, November 27: B12.

Siddins, Eileen, Ryan Daniel, and Robert Johnstone. 2016. "Building Visual Artists' Resilience Capabilities: Current Educator Strategies and Methods." *Journal of Arts & Humanities* 5 (7): 24–37.

Smith, Constance, and Sue Viders. 2007. *Art Office, 80+ Business Forms, Charts, Sample Letters, Legal Documents & Business Plans for Fine Artists*. 2nd ed. Nevada City, CA: Artnetwork.

Smithsonian Guidelines for Accessible Exhibition Design. www.si.edu/Accessibility/SGAED, accessed August 6, 2015, 17–26.

Sternberg, Robert J. 1997. "What Does It Mean to Be Smart?" *Educational Leadership* 54 (6): 99–109.

Sullivan, Graeme. 2004. "Studio Art as Research Practice." In *Handbook of Research and Policy in Art Education*. Edited by Elliot W. Eisner and Michael D. Day, 795–814. Mahwah, NJ: Lawrence Erlbaum.

Sutherland, Ian, and Sophia Krzys Acord. 2007. "Thinking with Art: From Situated Knowledge to Experiential Knowing." *Journal of Visual Art Practice* 6 (2): 125–40.

Tepper, Steven J. September 2016. "What Does It Mean to Sustain a Career in the Gig Economy?" In *Creativity Connects: Trends and Conditions Affecting U.S. Artists*. By Center for Cultural Innovation for Endowment for the Arts, 54–56. Washington, DC: National Endowment for the Arts.

Toor, Rachel. 2014. "Habits of Highly Productive Writers." *Chronicle of Higher Education*, November 21: A24–A25.

Utah Public Art Program & Utah Department of Environmental Quality. 2017. *Request for Artist Qualifications*. Salt Lake City: Utah Division of Arts & Museums.

Vitali, Julius. 2003. *The Fine Artist's Guide to Marketing and Self-Promotion*. New York: Allworth.

Weiss, Jeffrey. 2004. "Language in the Vicinity of Art: ARTISTS' WRITINGS, 1960–1975." *Artforum International* 42 (10): 212–17.

Wesch, Dianne H. B., Tamaki Onishi, Ruth H. DeHoog, and Sumera Syed. 2014. "Responding to the Needs and Challenges of Arts Entrepreneurs: An Exploratory Study of Arts Entrepreneurship in North Carolina Higher Education." *Artivate: A Journal of Entrepreneurship in the Arts* 3 (2): 21–37.

Zajonc, R. B., Sheila T. Murphy, and Marita Inglehart. 1989. "Feeling and Facial Efference: Implications of the Vascular Theory of Emotion." *Psychological Review* 96 (3): 395–416.